ASTRO CARTO GRAPHY

To my lodestars,
Paul and Libby

An astrologer's
guide to where
you'll thrive

ASTRO
CARTO
GRAPHY

Clarisse Monahan

CONTENTS

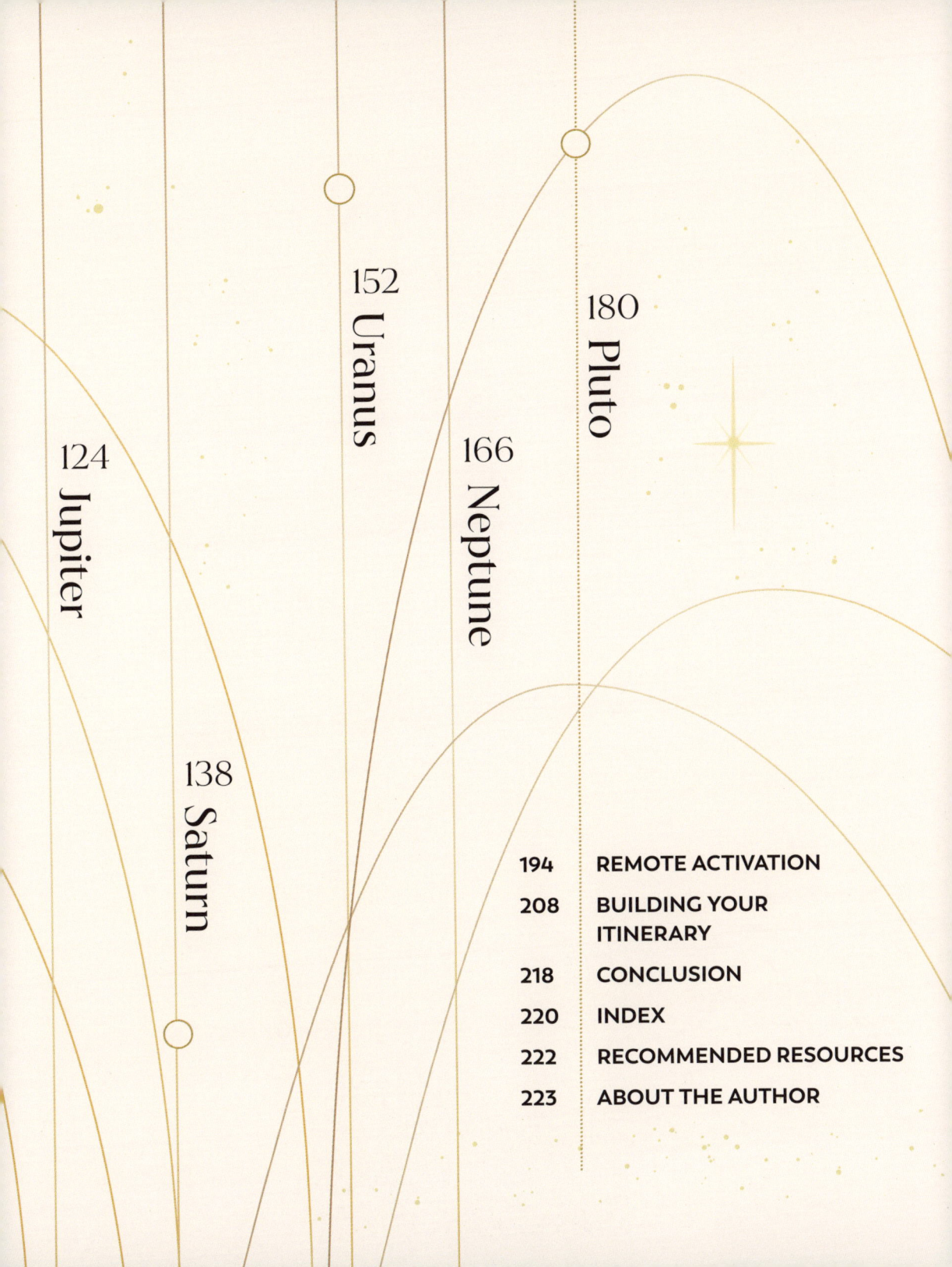

INTRODUCTION

The Importance of Elsewhere

This felicitous phrase is taken from the curmudgeonly, though brilliant, post-war poet Philip Larkin, whose verse – despite the gloomy night sky of its creator's sensibility – nonetheless dazzles and fascinates like its own kind of zodiac. While none of us has probably put it as well as Larkin, we all intuit the "importance of elsewhere" in our own lives. From taking a break from the familiar confines of home for a short weekend away, to travelling vast distances for work, pleasure, or love, we all feel elsewhere's insistence.

Why is "elsewhere" important? Larkin's reply to this is quite striking: "elsewhere" helps clarify who you are. It underwrites (or confirms) your very existence. Elsewhere, then, isn't just an exotic locale for pleasure-seeking and escape, but also for the profound work of self-understanding and personal development. On some level, you are reading this book, I would wager, because you intuit the importance of elsewhere for your own sense of self.

Not coincidentally, the stars themselves also recognize the importance of elsewhere. Indeed, what is known in astrology as the 9th house of your birth chart deals with travel, foreign lands, and broadening horizons. So, even the cosmos that gives your life its order invites and encourages you to get away. The questions become: to where? And when? And why? To find love? Success? New starts?

We can use the emerging field of astrocartography, which blends
astrology and geography, to provide an answer to these questions,
and to better realize which elsewhere suits us best.

While etymologically, astrocartography is a bit of a mouthful, it's
conceptually quite simple. Astrocartography – or locational astrology
– uses your unique birth chart to map personally auspicious or
challenging locations worldwide for romance, work, travel, family,
and more. I like to think of it as a kind of "Tinder for Places", which
matches us to our geographic hotspots. Just as we're compatible with
certain people, we likewise hit it off with certain cities, towns,
countries, or countrysides more than others. Montreal: yes. Rome:
not so much. Astrocartography can help explain these place-based
attractions. But how?

Over the course of this book, we will be examining the
fundamentals of astrocartography. From understanding planets
and their influence on us, to analysing your personalized
astrocartography (or star) map and interpreting what your
"planetary lines" might mean in the context of work, home,
relationships, and career, the ultimate goal here is to enrich your
life by activating your power places.

The Rise of Astrocartography

Although I've been studying, teaching, and lecturing about astrology for quite some time, it's only recently that I began to notice that my consultations started to involve more astrocartography requests.

Perhaps this intensified attention to "the importance of elsewhere" has been aided by remote working, which has enabled a kind of liberation from the drab trinity of job, commute, and mortgaged houses. No longer anchored to fixed longitudes and latitudes, people of all demographics are wanting to know how astrocartography can help them determine where best to live and thrive. Or perhaps the trend to valorize experience over things is driving generations to a new ethos of non-possessive individualism, where memories and connection to different cultures have become more important than hollow and unsustainable forms of materialism.

Whatever the sociological reasons for this surge of interest, this book hopes to edify people just getting into the topic of astrocartography.

A Recent History

The term "astrocartography" officially originated in the 1970s, coined by the renowned astrologer Jim Lewis. However, its roots can be traced back earlier in the 20th century, to the 1940s, when maps depicting eclipse paths first began to appear.

In the late 1950s, astrologer Donald Bradley created a map showing the positions of planets during the winter equinox of 1958. Later, in 1966, Cyril Fagan, another prominent astrologer, proposed the idea that different locations on Earth could be influenced by the positions of planets, suggesting that individuals might improve their lives by relocating to places where beneficial planetary energies were prominent. Fagan's proposal became the seed for "astrocartography".

The period from the 1970s to the 1990s saw significant advancements in astrology due to the development of computer software. Prior to this moment, the lack of precision in astrological calculations was a major limitation, as even small errors – just a few degrees off – could result in a profound misreading of a chart and the individual's cosmic profile. The advent of software revolutionized this, providing more accurate calculations and clearing up these ambiguities. Notably, Neil Michelsen and Michael Erlewine were pioneers in computerized astrology.

In 1975, Jim Lewis partnered with Gregg Howe of Astro Numeric Service to create the Astro*Carto*Graphy system, which people have been using for decades to generate insights into what locations their astrological power places might be. What set Lewis apart was his ability to create a system that helped people interpret their astrological maps. He listened to people's stories about their experiences in different locations and connected those to the qualities of various planets. Lewis made astromapping accessible and practical, allowing individuals to see how the stars could influence their lives based on where they lived.

Earlier Origins

Because I love the ancient astrologers – and feel we need to pay
homage to them wherever possible – it would be remiss to neglect
astrocartography's deeper roots. Indeed, one could argue that
while astrocartography is a relatively new term, it has always been
essential to the practice of astrology, which involves using your birth
time and where you were born to make predictions about your
cosmic destiny and direction. In what follows, I want to look briefly
at ways the power of place in older astrological systems has always
been a salient feature.

As with so many other fields of study, let's start with those
ever-clever Greeks, whose astrologers such as Ptolemy linked parts
of the Earth to the twelve zodiac signs (you'll learn more about these
on page 30). For Ptolemy, there were Piscean places, Ariean places,
Taurean places, and so on, and Greek astrologers would accordingly
suggest relocations to areas astrologically aligned with a person's
birth chart to enhance fortune and success. While modern
astrocartography focuses on planets (rather than Ptolemy's zodiac
signs), we nonetheless find in the Greek example the same spirit of
power places animating a deeper history of the topic.

In the context of Roman astrology, we encounter a markedly
darker use of locational astrology. Roman emperors and military
leaders (all imperialists) would consult astrologers when founding
colonies or moving soldiers to invade and conquer other lands.
Auspicious astrological conditions (which were auspicious for
the oppressors, but not so much the oppressed) were believed to
ensure the success and prosperity of new settlements. This example
suggests the bad seed version of the Greek system, using the power
of place to overpower people to exploit resources and territory.

While we can trace the lineaments of astrocartography across all
ancient cultures that practised astrology, the east Indian astrological

system known as Jyotish offers an intriguing wrinkle in its use of it. In Jyotish, certain directions are considered more auspicious than others. As such, entire Vedic (or ancient Indian) communities were organized architecturally around these energetic impulses. This was a practice known as Vastu Shastra, or "the science of architecture". Entering a city from the east, rather than from the south, ensured prosperity. In the context of Jyotish, we see how astrology was used, not so much to find a power place, but to literally construct one.

Despite their differences, however, common to all three instances was that astrocartography was used to determine a range of activities and practices to foster harmony, opportunity, and success (even if that "success" sometimes meant imperial oppression).

The Ptolemaic system illustrated by Andreas Cellarius, 1661

ASTROCARTOGRAPHY BASICS

Astrocartography in Action

So what are the mechanics of astrocartography? Without getting too technical, let's have a sneak peek at how it works.

Astrocartography maps your planetary lines longitudinally around the world. We will take a more detailed look at what this means using examples of an astrocartography map (or star map) on page 46, but for now, let's take a concrete situation involving Venus, the planet of love, romance, beauty, and desire.

Imagine you want to develop a travel itinerary that activates Venusian themes. You may be single and looking for romance, or you may be married and wanting to rekindle the passion. Based on your birth chart (see page 22), astrocartography would generate your unique Venus line and thereby locate numerous places on it that would sync you up with Planet Love's energy. These hotspots could be anywhere, like New York, Iceland, or the French Alps. While the closer you get to exact locales, the more powerful your activation, any distance up to 250 miles (400 kilometres) either side of a line is considered a power place.

Once you'd established potential destinations on your Venus line, you would then need to think about which of them resonates with you according to climate, culture, language, personal preferences, and activities. Iceland? Too remote. What about the West Village, New York City? That sounds better. Flight booked.

Having decided on a power place, you would then think through activities that align with the themes of your planet. As you plan your Venus line trip, you would want to engage in fun stuff that revolves, to some extent, around beauty, romance, love, and harmony. Scheduling a date at The Museum of Modern Art might, therefore, take precedence over waiting in long lines for a corndog at Coney Island. Alternatively, if travelling were not an option, you might remotely activate your power place by doing something to embody the energy of your power place from your current home, like watching a film shot in your power place (see more on pages 198–205).

What emerges from this whistle-stop tour is that astrocartography can help provide you with power places that resonate with you. But you also have to think about what your own preferences and needs are. They say you can lead a horse to water, but you can't make it drink. Something similar occurs with astrocartography: it can lead you to a range of places that will cosmically light up for you, but self-reflection is a crucial component in this process. Astrology and astrocartography, far from being deterministic systems, offer possibilities, or multiple-choice answers, where more than one can be correct.

Intersecting Lines

In our previous example, we imagined one planetary line running through a number of your power places: New York, Iceland, and the French Alps. Knowing that all these hotspots were astrocartographically auspicious for activating Venus energy, you engaged in some self-reflection and decided that New York would be the best for you at the moment.

But what if your unique birth chart – whose structuring dynamics we will learn about in more detail over pages 22–37 – presents a scenario where two or three planets cross through the same place? I've read many astrocartography charts, and this phenomenon happens quite frequently. For instance, you may not only have Venus running through New York, but lucky Jupiter, too. Interesting.

Harnessing the power of intersecting lines (or areas where multiple planetary influences cross) indicates another powerful strategy to maximize your experience within and around auspicious places. Intersecting planetary lines, especially when both planets are benefic (such as Jupiter and Venus) may intensify the positive qualities associated with each planet, lending an extraordinary energy to your vacation, extended stay, or relocation.

The flipside might be that we encounter places that lack power due to intersecting lines. The influence of Venus tends to bring beauty and love to our lives. But what if it intersects with the aggressive planet Mars in the French Alps? When Mars and Venus align, they create a charged mix of energies, combining tension and passion. This can lead to stress, confrontation, and emotional intensity, creating a combustive atmosphere.

However, that doesn't mean it's a bad place to visit. Mars represents action, so the Alps could be an ideal spot for an invigorating skiing or hiking trip, whether you're with a partner or flying solo. That way, you'll balance your Venusian need for connection with your Mars-driven thirst for adventure.

Harness the power of intersecting lines to maximize auspicious locations

Downloading Your Star Map

Now that you know how astrocartography works, it's time to generate your own astrocartography map (or star map). While your star map may look confusing at first, the next chapter (Decoding Your Star Map) will help you understand what your map means, and how these lines can be mobilized to empower yourself, your family, or your friends through astrocartography. To download your star map:

1. Go online to an astrocartography map generator. There are many of these, but I suggest using the AstroClick Travel feature on Astro.com.

2. Next, you'll be asked to enter your birth information. You will need accurate information regarding the day, hour, and minute of your birth, as well as the country and birth town in which you were born. Your birth time must be as close to accurate as possible, ideally within a ten-minute time period. Remember: things need to be as precise as possible.

3. Once you've entered your data, your generator will create your map. Once you have it, save it so that you can refer to it as often as you like throughout this book.

Astrology Fundamentals

In order to fully understand astrocartography (the study of how the cosmos determines your power places on Earth), we need to understand the basics of astrology (the study of how the motions of planets through the sky impact your life).

Astrology is the study of how things far away in our Solar System – such as the Moon, Jupiter, the Sun, and the other planets – affect things close to us such as our friendships, personalities, likes and dislikes, and career. Or, to put it another way, astrology studies how the astronomical positions of the planets' and the motions of these planets affect macro and microscopic events on Earth.

Just like weather patterns, these planetary motions create sunny seasons in our personal lives, or ones that are partly cloudy with a chance of rain. As such, each planet has cosmic energies associated with it. When a planet transits (moves through the sky), these energies can be felt in different ways (see page 206).

Certain astrological transits involving Mars (the planet of war) can make you feel at war with yourself or others; transits involving Jupiter (the planet of abundance) can lead to windfalls and new opportunities; and some transits involving Saturn (the planet of less) can cause you loss or difficulty.

It is by tracing these movements and transits of the planets through the sky that astrologers can start to learn about when auspicious and inauspicious times are coming, both on the level of collective life, and on the level of an individual. And the way that astrologers access these predictive powers is through a birth chart.

Our objective over the remainder of this chapter therefore is to familiarize you with the fundamentals of your unique astrological birth chart.

Your Birth Chart

I like to think of a birth chart as a kind of cosmic portrait, taken the moment you were born into this universe. Your birth chart tells you where a planet like Mercury was in the sky the moment you entered the universe. And based on this birth chart intel, your star map (see page 46) shows where your Mercury hotspots are on Earth. Two maps, one sky.

Your birth chart is the key to your astrological identity. It helps you understand your personality, behavioural patterns, and preferences. Every birth chart is made up of three components: the ten astrological planets; the twelve zodiac signs; and the twelve houses. But despite these shared features, your birth chart is unique; just like a fingerprint, no two people's charts are exactly the same.

For example, if you were born at 6am in Beijing on 1 March 1991, your Sun will be in the zodiac sign of watery Pisces; your Moon will be in practical Virgo; and Venus will be in firey Aries. The way the energetic impulses of the planets combine with the zodiac signs sets your cosmic personality in motion, helping to dictate your relation to (among other things) money, routine, health, recreation, creativity, and romance.

However, this Beijing cosmic portrait will be very different to someone born in Lagos on 13 December, 1997, at 3:40pm, where planets will be in different places, at different degrees (or points of emphasis), and in different signs. In the Beijing portrait, the Sun's location may make you more prone to desire things of the spiritual nature, whereas the Lagos portrait may make you desire more intellectual pursuits.

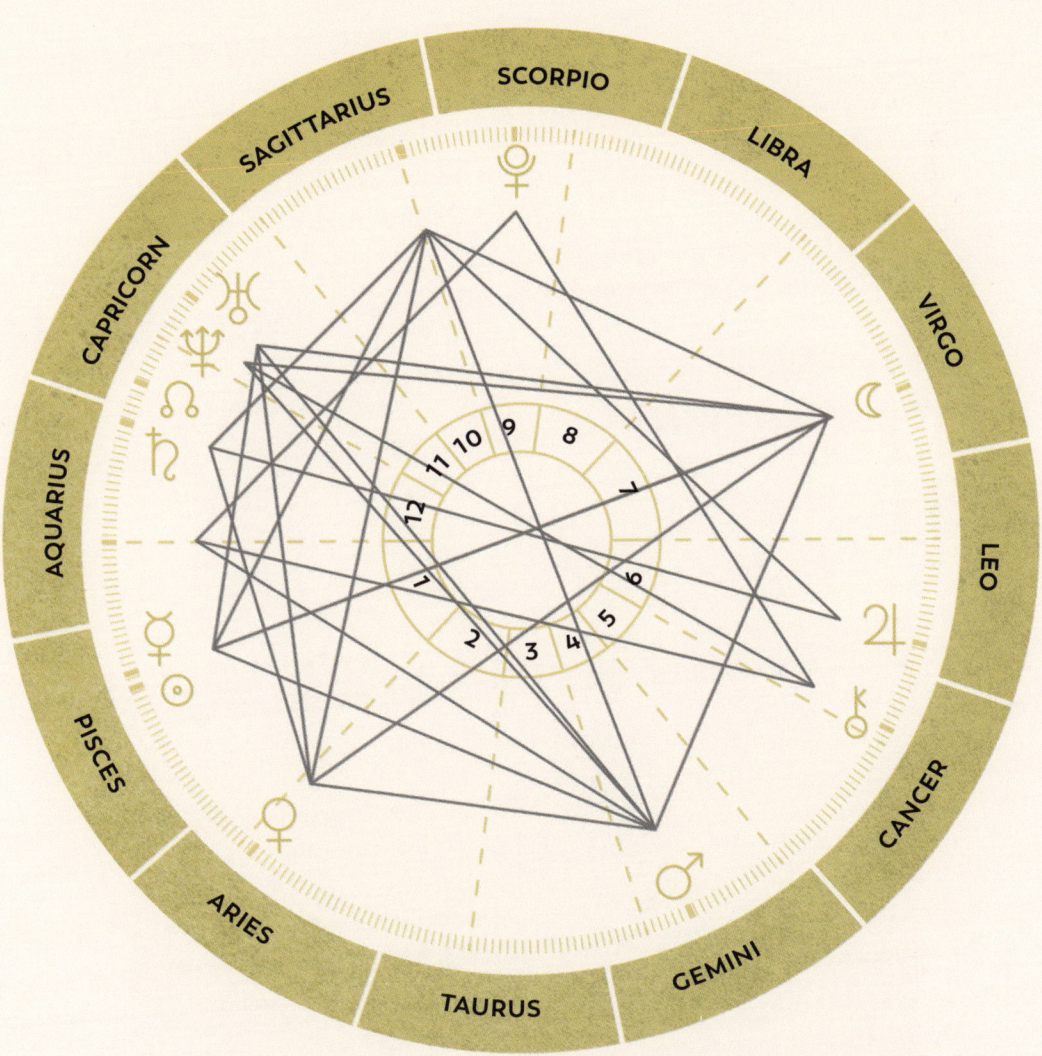

Birth chart of someone born on 1 March 1991, 6:00am, Beijing

The Planets

As a birth chart is a picture of the location of the planets at our time and place of birth, it is essential for us to familiarize ourselves with the basic significations of each planet when we want to figure out our astrocartography lines, or power places.

Let's start with the planet closest to the Sun – Mercury – and move further away from there, before discussing the Moon and Sun.

MERCURY

Known as the messenger planet, Mercury governs over communication or relays between people and things in our world. Mercury is related to intellect, powers of speech, precision, and the conversation between people. Mercury in a birth chart determines how we express ourselves. A planet is considered strong when it is located in one of the signs it rules, and a strong Mercury in your birth chart may manifest as having a way with words.

VENUS

Known as "Planet Love", Venus governs over romance, desire, beauty, and social harmony. It looks like a diamond in the sky, glittering eternally like an engagement ring on the finger of God. It influences our heart and attracts people to each other. In a birth chart, Venus determines how we give and receive love. A strong Venus in your birth chart may manifest as easily attracting admirers.

MARS

If Venus is about love, Mars is more about strife. It's the planet that speaks to confrontation, argumentation, and competition. Also known as the "Red Planet" for the way it glows forever hot, Mars drives us forward. But this drive often comes into conflict with others. In our birth chart, Mars determines what we fight for and against. A strong Mars in your birth chart may manifest as being self-assertive and ambitious.

JUPITER

As we move further out in the cosmos, we encounter Jupiter. Astrologers call this planet the "Luck Giver". It's the planet that makes life feel bigger, richer, and more abundant. By far the largest planet in our Solar System, it's also the planet that pumps us up with confidence and tends to send opportunities your way during its major transits through your chart.

SATURN

Just as Mars (the planet of war) is a kind of antihero to Venus (the planet of love), Saturn cosmically opposes Jupiter. Saturn relates to structure, restriction, discipline, law, and order, and tends to confine, whereas Jupiter expands. We need Saturn to give order to our lives, but sometimes, during its transits, we can feel a bit too locked down. In your birth chart, Saturn can bring challenges but also long-term rewards.

URANUS

Literally one of our most out-there planets (it is the third furthest planet from the Sun), the energy of Uranus is likewise "out there", as in strange, unexpected, and quirky. It's a planet that introduces the element of surprise into our cosmic order, allowing us to think outside the box or approach problems in unconventional ways to generate new solutions.

NEPTUNE

Neptune is named after the Roman god of the sea, and is related to spiritual transcendence, and going beyond the material world. It impacts dreams and our spiritual yearnings. During its transits, we can feel more inspired artistically, or tend to fantasize about alternate ways of living and being. Your Neptune sign reflects the part of you that's dreamy, intuitive, and sometimes lost in illusions. It's where your creativity and inspiration thrive, but also where you might overlook reality.

PLUTO

The slowest moving planet in the Solar System (as it takes 248 years to orbit the Sun), Pluto indicates revolutionary change and new beginnings. Mythologically, Pluto is associated with Hades, lord of the underworld. Accordingly, Pluto in your birth chart shows where you undergo deep transformation and face hidden truths. It pushes you to confront what you'd rather avoid, driving profound change and growth.

SUN

The Sun and the Moon are technically not planets, but astrologers will often use that term to designate our two "luminaries". The Sun is related to vitality. It brings life, makes us feel alive, and, importantly, makes us feel seen, visible, and appreciated. The Sun represents our social self. During Sun transits, social recognition tends to occur, as well as social advancement. In your birth chart, the Sun determines how you act in the world based on ego-needs.

MOON

The Moon governs over your emotional processing in your birth chart. It helps explain why some people handle adversity with great aplomb, while others may get vexed by even the smallest disturbance in their little corner of the world. If the Sun shines light on our public path, the Moon lights up the way we feel about the path we are on. A strong Moon in your birth chart may manifest in things like heightened intuition.

SUN (the planet of ego) Relates to public self, ego, vitality

MERCURY (the messenger planet) Governs communication and conveyances

VENUS (the planet of love) Relates to love, beauty, romance, desire

MOON (the planet of feelings) Governs our emotions, intuitions, and moods

MARS (the planet of war) Governs drive, ambition and confrontation

PLUTO (the bulldozer planet) Governs revolutionary change, major transformation, and creation through destruction

NEPTUNE (the planet of fantasy) Relates to mystical visions, art, dreams, glamour, and illusions

URANUS (the planet of strange happenings) Rules innovation, surprise, and unexpected phenomena

SATURN (the planet of less) Relates to discipline, challenges, law, order, and structure

JUPITER (the planet of abundance) Relates to luck, opportunities, and expansion

The Zodiac

In the Western astrological system, the sky is divided into twelve equal parts, each corresponding to one of the twelve constellations (or signs of the zodiac).

It takes the Sun about a year to move through the whole zodiac, spending about a month in each zodiac sign. Libra season, for example, corresponds to a time period each year when the Sun moves through that constellation (from approximately 23 September to 22 October). During Libra season, the qualities and energy associated with that sign become more activated in your life. Given that Libra's symbol is the scales, you may find it easier to find balance between friends, partners, or family and your needs.

Each zodiac sign has a symbol, element, and set of meanings, traits, and characteristics. Let's look into these cosmic qualities in more detail.

ARIES
(21 March
to 19 April)

Notorious for its hot-headedness and ruled by war-like Mars, Aries energy is fiery and ambitious. As the first sign in the zodiac, Aries is the "baby" of the group. It influences us to be bold, impulsive, loyal, and protective.

Keywords: Bold, ambitious, independent, at times brash and reckless
Ruling Planet: Mars | **Element:** Fire | **Symbol:** The Ram

TAURUS
(20 April
to 20 May)

Ruled by luxury-loving Venus, Taurus energy is earthy and steady. It's also associated with the finer things. Think instead black car service, caviar, and cashmere. Taurus also provides a sense of security, and is especially domestic.

Keywords: Reliable, patient, practical, sensual, at times overly indulgent
Ruling Planet: Venus | **Element:** Earth | **Symbol:** The Bull

GEMINI
(21 May
to 20 June)

Ruled by communications expert Mercury, Gemini energy is quick, brilliant, and social. As an air sign, Geminis are known for their gift of persuasion, their imaginative minds, and their ever-curious souls.

Keywords: Adaptable, curious, loquacious, catty, at times glib
Ruling Planet: Mercury | **Element:** Air | **Symbol:** The Twins

CANCER
(21 June
to 22 July)

Ruled by the Moon and always up in its feelings, Cancer is a nurturing water sign associated with emotionality. Cancer energy influences us to be near family and to stay inside more, and prefers privacy to publicity.

Keywords: Nurturing, sensitive, compassionate, at times moody
Ruling Planet: Moon | **Element:** Water | **Symbol:** The Crab

LEO
(23 July
to 22 August)

Ruled by the kingly Sun, Leo energy is about being seen in the spotlight. As a fire sign, Leo loves its pride of friends, so long as it gets the lion's share of attention.
Keywords: Confident, charismatic, at times self-centred
Ruling Planet: Sun | **Element:** Fire | **Symbol:** The Lion

VIRGO
(23 August
to 22 September)

Virgo energy is precise and diligent. As an earth sign, it's also associated with practicality. Ruled by the analytical side of Mercury, Virgo influences us to be highly ordered.
Keywords: Analytical, perfectionistic, practical, at times fussy
Ruling Planet: Mercury | **Element:** Earth | **Symbol:** The Virgin

LIBRA
(23 September
to 22 October)

An air sign, Libra energy manifests in deliberate action that seeks to balance multiple viewpoints and build consensus. Ruled by Venus, Libra's essence is to create harmony.
Keywords: Diplomatic, consensus-building, fair, at times indecisive
Ruling Planet: Venus | **Element:** Air | **Symbol:** The Scales

SCORPIO
(23 October
to 21 November)

Ruled by war-like Mars, watery Scorpio's energy tends to get us fixated on things. It's the Sherlock Holmes of the zodiac, doing its detective work to get to the bottom of situations. It can make us somewhat sharp or stinging in our dealings with the world and search for truth.
Keywords: Intense, passionate, strategic, at times obsessive
Ruling Planet: Mars | **Element:** Water | **Symbol:** The Scorpion

SAGITTARIUS

(22 November
to 21 December)

Ruled by generous Jupiter, fiery Sagittarius is either out looking for trouble on the Vegas strip, or at home in its study, pondering higher truths – such is their dual nature. Sagittarius energy can make us prone to adventure, risk, and ribaldry, or it can influence us to contemplate our existence.

Keywords: Adventurous, risk-taking, philosophical, opinionated
Ruling Planet: Jupiter | **Element:** Fire | **Symbol:** The Archer

CAPRICORN

(22 December
to 19 January)

Serious and Saturn-ruled, Capricorn is an earth sign whose influence turns us to the things of the world, such as commerce, business, and mercantilism. Capricorn is a no-nonsense, practical energy.

Keywords: Disciplined, commercially minded, hardworking, at times cold
Ruling Planet: Saturn | **Element:** Earth | **Symbol:** The Goat

AQUARIUS

(20 January
to 18 February)

Known for loving all things new, innovative, and forward-thinking, Aquarius energy influences us to favour big-picture problem solving. Ruled by Saturn, this cerebral air sign can sometimes seem detached from the world as it tries to figure it out.

Keywords: Innovative, progressive, humanitarian, aloof
Ruling Planet: Saturn | **Element:** Air | **Symbol:** The Water Bearer

PISCES

(19 February
to March 20)

Pisces is a water sign ruled by generous Jupiter. Its energy pushes us toward greater demonstrations of compassion, spiritual seeking, artistic achievement, and empathy. The quintessential Pisces energy is feeling too much.

Keywords: Empathetic, dreamy, spiritual, at times overly-sensitive
Ruling Planet: Jupiter | **Element:** Water | **Symbol:** The Fishes

The Astrological Houses

There are twelve houses in everyone's birth chart, and each one corresponds to some essential, universal aspect of our lives, such as love, friendship, money, and career. Just as everyone has the same ten planets transiting through the twelve zodiac signs, everyone has twelve houses in their birth chart. What makes your birth chart unique is the way that the zodiac signs and planets fall into these houses and interact with each other.

Understanding more about what the different houses mean in your birth chart and which planets fall into them can help you begin working out which areas to focus on, and the best power places in which to do so.

1st SELF AND IDENTITY

The first house is the most powerful house, as it is connected to your cosmic identity. This is the part of a birth chart that reveals how we appear to others, and how we think about ourselves and the world. When war-like Mars is placed there, we get personality types that can be internally conflicted. Mercury finds its joy here however, as it can convey a person who can communicate their words clearly and with alacrity.

2nd MONEY

This house refers to profits, goods, value, and possessions. Restrictive Saturn here on a birth chart could represent a life of limited cash, while expansive Jupiter here could suggest a person more likely to find fortune. Reckless Mars doesn't do well here, portending risky financial behaviour, while Mercury indicates shrewdness.

3rd COMMUNICATION

All manner of communication relates to the 3rd house, which also governs over short journeys. Mercury in this house indicates precision with words, while expansive Jupiter can point toward prolific writers. This house also relates to siblings, cousins, and neighbours. Belligerent Mars in this house could predict difficult relationships.

4th HOME

This house deals with land, property, and legacy. Expansive Jupiter here could suggest luck with real estate. Conversely, restrictive Saturn in this house might betoken challenges with finding properties or encountering living situations burdened by excessive rules and regulations, either with roommates or partners.

5th ROMANCE

This house deals with fun, romance, creation, recreation, and procreation. It's also associated with nightlife, pleasures, and taverns.

Venus has a good time in this part of the chart, as it indicates desire and pleasure, while dour Saturn might not, drying up the seeds of creation.

ROUTINE, HEALTH, AND DIET

The sixth house signifies diet, routine, busy work, and health. It also pertains to our work environment, employees, pets, and habits. Mars in this house is auspicious because it loves putting its high energy to use, and Saturn can thrive here too with its focus on order and structure.

RELATIONSHIPS

This house deals with business, partnerships, marriages, relationships, sweethearts, and questions of love. The Moon in this house on a birth chart may indicate a person who feels moonstruck towards their partner(s), while Mars can indicate power struggles. Venus and Jupiter transit, in contrast, can indicate understanding and harmony.

DEBTS

This house relates to financial debts, wills, legacies, and last testament, as well as death, sex, taxes, and spiritual transformation. Ultimately, there is an occult, dark, intuitive energy to this house. Venus in this house can suggest a sexual kink, and Pluto's focus on the unconscious can make for an intense character when found here on a birth chart.

SPIRITUALITY, KNOWLEDGE, AND DISTANT LANDS

The ninth house takes the mind or body from common to higher places, either physically in a life-altering journey overseas, or mentally through knowledge, books, and spiritual insight. Jupiter here indicates a person who likes studying abroad or expanding their horizons. The Sun has its joy here, too, as the Sun and knowledge are connected to the mind.

10th CAREER

This house deals with career and public persona. It also pertains to profession and vocation, honours, and awards. Sad Saturn in a chart here can deny professional recognition, while expansive Jupiter and the Sun can increase it. This is the house of striving.

11th FRIENDSHIP

The eleventh house concerns our friends, associates, and social networking. It also deals with betrayals, trust, and confidence, too. Jupiter in a chart here tends to portend someone who finds good luck through acquaintances (for example, getting a job due to someone they know). Venus, a social planet, also sits well here, while Mars can imply conflict and in-fighting in such relationships.

12th SECRETS

This is the house of secrets, the unconscious, dreams, and sleep. Everything about this house is in the shadows. Grim Saturn, maker of mischiefs, can be fortuitous when placed here, while Pluto here can symbolize a person who will need to do some work to let go of emotional baggage for spiritual growth.

DECODING YOUR STAR MAP

Your Star Map

Now that you're more familiar with your birth chart, you can start to explore where its planetary influences are strongest for you in the world on your star map. This is the essence of astrocartography. Combining astrology and geography, it helps you find power places for your career, relationships, home, and self-development, which are collectively known as your big four. But how so exactly? This is the big question of the chapter. To answer it, let's have a look at a star map.

When you download your star map (see page 19), you'll get something that looks like the map on page 46. As you can see, the thing is a bit of a mess, with lines of different colours cascading and crisscrossing the globe.

You'll also see four groups of letters at the top of the map – AC, DC, IC, and MC – along with symbols attached to the letters. While this initially seems confusing, once you know how to decode these lines and letters, you will be well on your way to grasping astrocartography.

Planetary Lines

To begin decoding your star map, let's look at just one line to start. This single line represents one of your astrological planets, and is called a planetary line.

At the top of this map, you will see a symbol and the letters MC, both of which tell us crucial information about this planetary line in particular. In this example, the symbol represents the Sun (but each planet has its own unique glyph). You will also see the letters MC, which stands for Medium Coeli – Latin for "middle of the sky". Thus, this planetary line shows where the Sun was culminating at the moment you were born.

As you will learn on pages 55–67, the locations along the Sun line suggest a particular kind of power place for you.

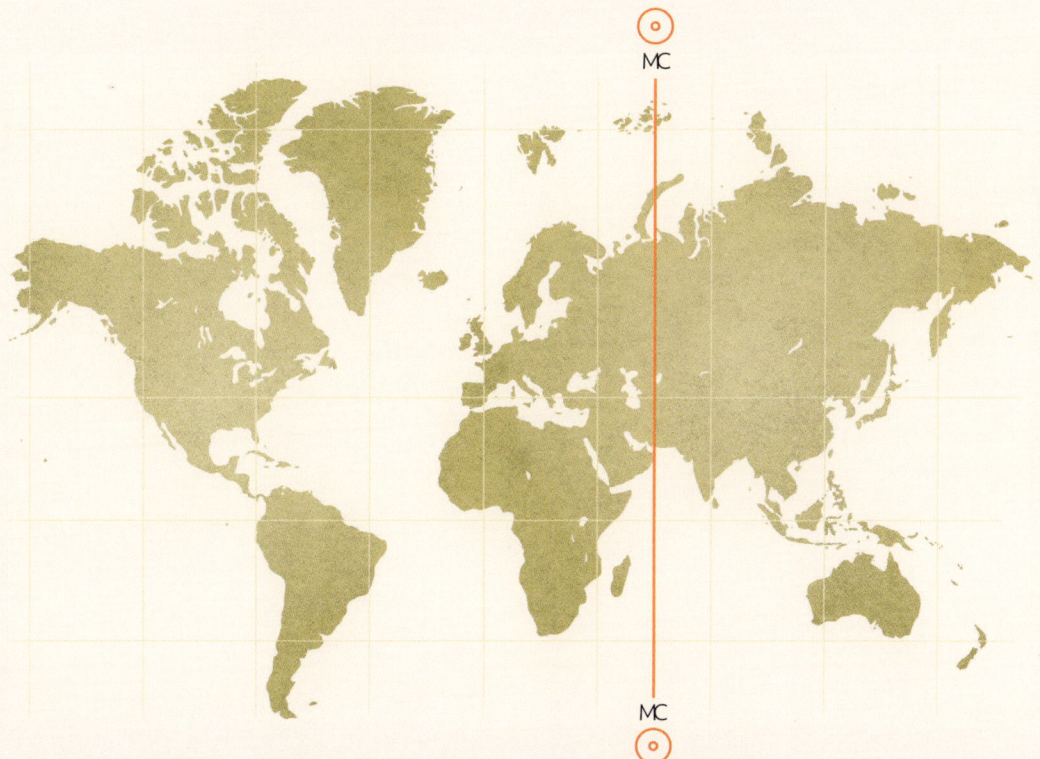

Now, let's add a second line to your star map, which clearly runs through different places than the first. Accordingly, if you look to the top of this new line, you will observe the same Sun symbol, but with the letters IC, rather than MC. This new line indicates that the Sun was at its lowest point the moment of your birth. IC stands for Imum Coeli (Latin for "bottom of the sky") and the locations that run alongside this Sun line indicate a second set of potential power places. MC Sun line cities will have a different energy and meaning for you than those of the IC Sun line.

Even with just a couple of planetary lines, this is a lot to digest. But so far, we have successfully identified the three main components of your astrocartography map: the lines designate the planet; the symbols tell you which planet you are looking at; and the letters refer to the planet's position in the sky when you were born.

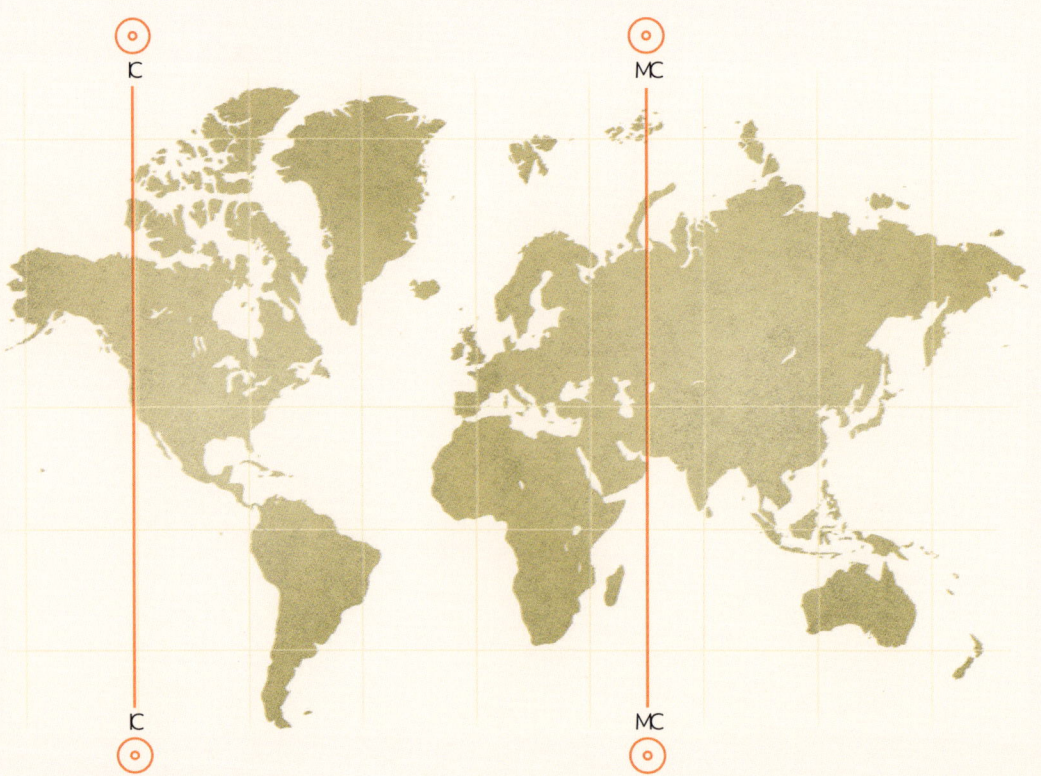

SUN

MOON

MERCURY

VENUS

MARS

JUPITER

SATURN

URANUS

NEPTUNE

PLUTO

Angularity

Imagine that you were born in Beijing at noon. From your perspective, the Sun would have been at its highest point in the sky. But at the same time, the Sun would also be rising in Dublin, setting in LA, while the night would be at its darkest point in Buenos Aires, half a world away. The moment you were born, the Sun was rising, setting, peaking, and anti-culminating somewhere relative to you. These four different positions are what's known as angularity in astrocartography. All planets have these four planetary positions, and these planetary positions will help provide you with insight into where your hotspots are for your big four (personal development, relationships, career, and home).

THE FOUR POSITIONS

AC (or ascending) refers to the rising of a planet. The AC lines on your star map are your personal lines.

DC (or descending) refers to the setting of a planet. The DC lines on your star map are your relationship lines.

MC (or Medium Coeli) is when a planet is peaking. The MC lines on your star map are your career lines.

IC (or Imum Coeli) refers to the planet's darkest or furthest point from where it is peaking (also known as anti-culminating). The IC lines on your star map are your home lines.

In this image, we see the four lines for the Sun (corresponding to its four positions of angularity), and we can also see the four Jupiter lines. Notice how the locations on these Jupiter lines differ from those of the Sun lines, representing a new set of potential power places related to Jupiterian (rather than solar) energy.

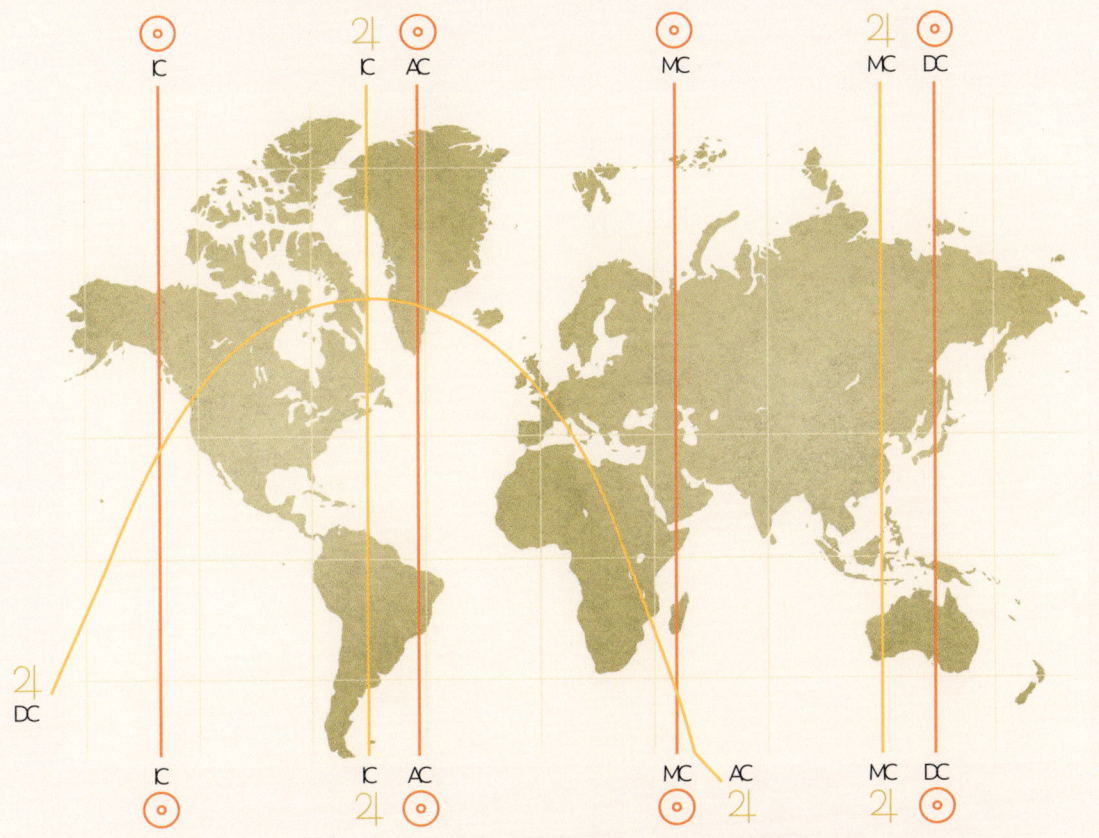

Now that we know there are four lines for each of the ten planets on every star map, it starts to make sense why it initially looks so complex. That's 40 planetary lines uniquely interlacing on just one map.

The rest of this chapter will begin to explore how these lines, based off of their angularity, represent profound aspects of our personal development, relationships, career, and home life.

A Full
Star Map

Star map for someone
born at 9:00am on
20 March 2025,
London, UK

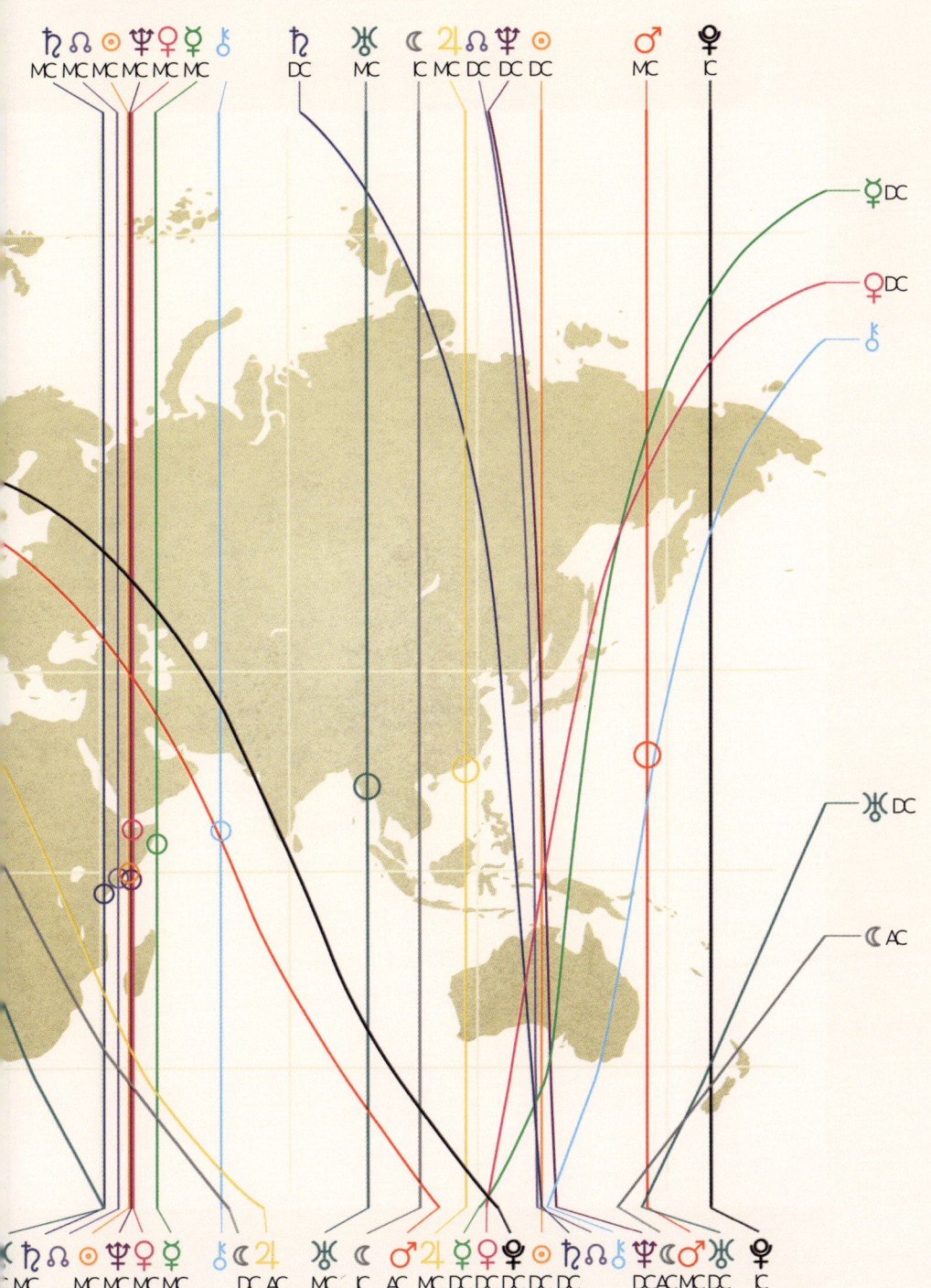

The AC Line – The Personal Line

The AC line refers to when and where a given planet was rising relative to your time and place of birth. When the Sun rises, we call it dawn. But here's the thing: all of the planets rise. In your unique star map, each planet has its dawn position, so to speak, or its own rising energy, and the locations along this dawn-like planetary horizon line indicate potential power places for you.

Symbolically, this rising energy influences your self-identity, outward appearance, and the first impressions you make on others. It determines how you engage with the world, how you initiate actions, and how others perceive you. This line is most associated with your personality. When you go to power places on a planet's AC line, you enliven that planet's energy in your life, particularly in terms of self-expression and personal growth. Locations on the AC planetary lines can feel invigorating, offering opportunities for self-discovery and new beginnings. Spending time in a place where a planet is on this line might make you feel more alive and true to yourself.

However, not all planetary AC lines have the same energy, power, and influence. For instance, if you go to a location on your Venus AC line, it will tend to enhance Venusian qualities related to your sense of self (see page 102). This is where you may feel more charm, attractiveness, and social grace. Such an experience will differ greatly from locations on the Mars AC line. Power places along this axis will tend to stimulate Martian energy. You may feel more self-assertion or ambition for pursuing personal goals, so you might go to a location on your Mars AC if you want to enliven an action-oriented side to your personality (see page 116).

The DC Line – The Relationship Line

The DC line refers to when and where a planet was setting (or descending) relative to your time and place of birth. Just as planets rise, they also set, and when you were born, every planet was setting somewhere. The hotspots along your DC lines indicate potential power places for you, but unlike the ego-driven AC lines, the DC lines are energetically connected to the Other, partnerships, romance, and social interaction. In opposition to the AC lines, which encourage you to focus on yourself, DC lines encourage collaboration, compromise, and the understanding of your place in relation to others.

Power places on your DC lines tend to enliven a spirit of cooperation, the desire for romance, or the search for a soulmate. Living on or visiting one of your DC lines could make you feel more selfless, and suggests an energy that inspires you to give rather than get, offering opportunities for nurturing relationships or meaningful romantic encounters.

Power places on the Saturn DC line might point to sites where you learn the importance of commitment and responsibility (see page 144). This will be a much different experience than, say, power places along the Jupiter DC line, which might be ideal for expanding your social circle, forming beneficial partnerships, or experiencing growth through relationships.

DC lines emphasize the importance of others in your life. They might be where you meet significant people who influence your path or where you learn valuable lessons about collaboration, compromise, and connection. Ultimately, your DC lines function as the inverse of your AC lines; they're where you can go for romance and relationships, while your AC lines are places for self-exploration and me-time.

The MC Line – The Career Line

The MC line (or Midheaven) designates where a planet was peaking in the sky relative to when and where you were born. When you were born, each planet was peaking somewhere in the sky, and the locations along your MC line point to potential power places for you centred around work, calling, professional aspirations, and public recognition.

Planets at their Midheaven are at their most visible, so our MC lines are about outward achievement, how we shine and succeed in the public sphere, and where we ourselves are most visible. When you align with power places on your MC lines, you may be more drawn to award-seeking and honours. Reputation might also take on more importance. Going to a hotspot on one of your MC lines can raise your profile or bring you more into view on social media or at work. While that can sound attractive to some people, remember that bright lights invite scrutiny.

Power places on your Mercury MC line (see page 92) will tend to be all about communication, trade, hustle, and moving and shaking. Compare this experience to the Moon MC line, where careers tend to be less about making money and more about doing work that aligns with your inner moral compass, or with causes that you feel deeply about. On your Moon MC line (see page 78), you would want to be recognized for the care, love, or passion you put into a project rather than your KPIs.

Just as your AC and DC line form a pair of opposites, your MC line (the most public-facing of your big four) finds its opposite in the private energy of the IC line (our most private of the big four).

The IC Line – The Home Line

The IC line stands for Imum Coeli, which derives from Latin, meaning "bottom of the sky". When you were born, each planet was anti-culminating somewhere in the sky, and symbolically, the power places on your IC lines represent where you might feel a sense of comfort, security, and belonging. It's about home, and your IC lines speak to where you want to become invisible, or want to only be seen by those closest to you.

Visiting or living in a location on an IC line will also increase your desire to get in touch with your roots, or to put down new ones by starting, growing, or nurturing your own family. This line is connected, therefore, to healing energy.

Locations on your Moon IC line might be particularly fecund sites to start or grow a family, reconnect with loved ones, and settle down to the world of domestic comforts—nesting, kids' soccer games, dinners around large tables massed with foison from the harvest, creative projects that allow you to express your inner self.

Conversely, power places on your Mercury IC line (see page 92) might suggest sites where you can enliven communication between family, parents, and children, or where you increase activity in or around the house. As Mercury pertains to communication and hustle energy, your Mercury IC line, accordingly, would have a bustle to it, and, consequently, home life on it might feel busier in the garden, kitchen, and boudoir.

Of your big four, you IC lines are the places you go to for restoration, retreat, and rejuvenation, and it functions as the opposite to your Midheaven. It is ultimately your home line, where you most belong.

THE PLANET
LINES

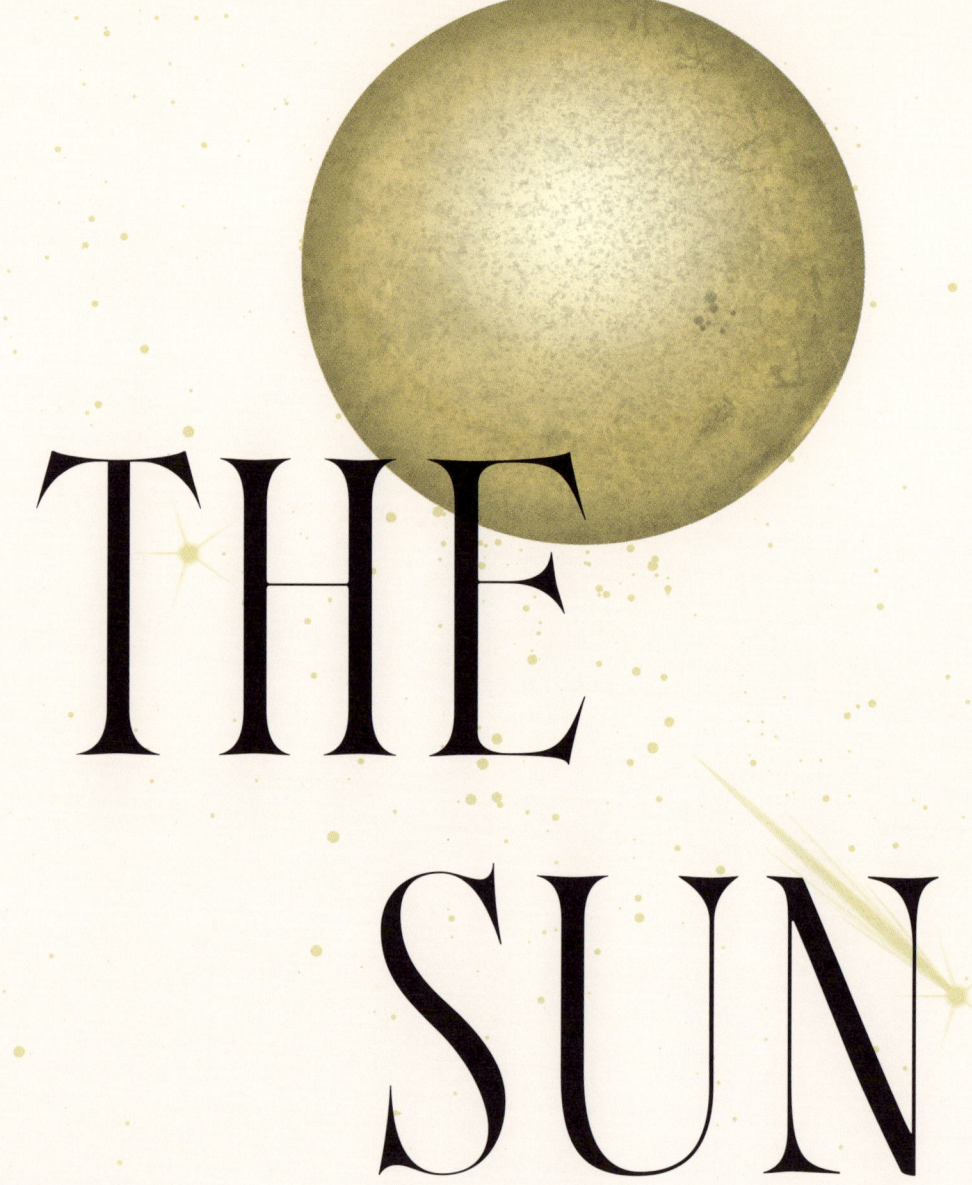

THE
SUN

Confidence | Leadership
Creativity | Personal Growth

The Sun line maps power places where you may better demonstrate confidence, strength, and leadership, especially related to public life, career, and calling. Those living on or visiting locations along their Sun line may feel more physical and professional vitality, attract social recognition, and develop a reputation for expertise in their given field. While the Sun line may lead to arrogance, it ultimately brings clarity, purpose, and self-motivation to your career, as well as increased energy for relationships.

The Planet of Ego

Most people know their Sun (or star) sign, even if they don't know more about astrology than that. When we claim "I'm a Libra" or "I'm an Aquarius", we are basically saying that the Sun was transiting through a given constellation in the sky on the day we were born.

Because the Sun illumines and activates our zodiac sign, it's connected to our ego, sense of self, and identity. The Sun dominates astrology, just as it dominates our heavens. It helps us align with who we are, or who we want to be, and helps us answer questions like: what do I want? What do I need? And how do I get there?

The Sun's Light Qualities

Heliotropism refers to a phenomenon in botany that involves the turning (tropism) of plants towards the sunlight (helios). This term can also be used to describe the Sun; it's an industrious energy, eager to rule and exert power – but in a prudent way. As the Sun is associated with vitality, it manifests in an energy that is faithful, sound in judgement, majestic, and steady. It also bolsters confidence, helping us to swagger into bars or boardrooms.

The Sun's Shadow Qualities

Because the Sun relates to ego and identity (and because it often provides you with more self-confidence and executive presence), its darker qualities can also manifest in an overly plump sense of self-regard, which can lead to arrogance, or worse, out-sized narcissism. It can also lead to showing off due to a need to be the centre of attention, and symbolize an overly fierce sense of independence.

Life on the Sun Line

Glowing. Confident. Bold. On the Sun line, people will turn to you for answers, guidance, leadership, advice, and decisions.

Those who visit or relocate to their Sun line tend to feel like they are shining brightly and attracting attention in the public sphere or through an online persona.

Like the life-giving force of the Sun, this line is associated with vitality, where you have more energy for your own life-purpose, as well as relationships, home, and career. Those on their Sun line also tend to speak of finally seeing more clearly where they are going in their lives, especially as it pertains to professional endeavours and career. And it makes sense; the Sun illuminates our world, and, by aligning with your solar power places, you may likewise see your own world in a powerful new light.

TRAVELLING ON YOUR SUN LINE

BEST FOR
reconnecting with yourself
if you're feeling lost; building
confidence; getting some attention;
finding an energy boost after illness
or a period of low energy; generating
vitality; healing after a setback;
or embracing a more vibrant
social persona.

WHAT TO PLAN
activities that let you
shine in the Sun, like surfing
classes; volleyball; picnicking;
or anything where you can
absorb Vitamin D.

WHAT TO PACK
standout outfits and
sunglasses; bling; gold items
so you can better reflect the
Sun's splendour; citrine crystals;
and William Finnegan's *Barbarian
Days*, the most gorgeous book
ever written about life in the
surf and sun.

The Sun
AC ———— Personal Line

When you're travelling to or living on your Sun personal line, you will feel more brilliant, confident, and like a superhero. This, in turn, impacts how others perceive you, as they will see you as charismatic, dynamic, and full of life.

While this line can amplify your superpowers, it may also make you somewhat ego-centric (on some level, most superheroes are). As such, care may need to be taken to mitigate against this, as you can't always be out saving the city from villains. Balance is required on the Sun personal line, so while you shine and save the world, make sure you also embrace calming yoga techniques and coffee with friends.

ENGAGE IN CREATIVE PURSUITS

To develop yourself on this line, try to be more open to creative activities like art, writing, music, or performance to help you express yourself. Taking classes or workshops to enhance your skills in these areas is especially auspicious on this line.

GET FEEDBACK

While you can expect your charisma and confidence to flourish, you should also endeavour to seek constructive feedback from trusted friends or mentors who can provide valuable insights. Learning to appreciate and grow from constructive criticism will help keep your ego in check.

AVOID VANITY PROJECTS

Expect to be more invested in your image and your physical appearance on this line. But, to avoid your life becoming a vanity project, work on developing emotional intelligence to help you navigate relationships effectively. Empathize. Sympathize. Be a mirror to others (rather than merely gazing at your own reflection).

The Sun

DC ——————— Relationship Line

The Sun relationship line will tend to attract those who want you to shine, especially regarding your career aspirations. This is not a line for needy partners who resent your hustle. Instead, this is a line where you and your significant other are allowed to be your most self-sufficient selves, while supporting each other's development.

And it's not just about you (even if the Sun line tends to make it seem like it is). The kind of respect and admiration your partner shows for your self-assertion needs to be reciprocated here, especially as you will tend to be attracted to stronger personalities. On your Sun power places for relationships, you're not looking for someone in a supporting role. Rather, you should be looking for a co-star with their own charisma and magical on-screen presence.

EMBRACE POWER COUPLEDOM

The Sun line is all about shine, and in the context of relationships, this means solar power places will tend to attract partners who are high-achieving, confident, and career-oriented. Expect a dynamic relationship here where you are happy to see the other succeed and vice versa.

BEWARE OF POWER STRUGGLES

Given that the Sun line can unduly boost self-esteem, you
might need to prepare for ego-clashes and power struggles.
All relationships have these, but they may be more
pronounced on this line.

PUBLIC DISPLAYS OF AFFECTION

Don't be afraid to be more public and expressive as you
bask in the mutual reflections of each other's love on this
line. Just as the Sun's visibility can't be denied, Sun line
relationships tend to be bold, confident, and out in the
public eye or at the centre of social gatherings.

The Sun

Career Line

The Sun represents our most public-facing energy, illuminating our outer world of social life with its competitions, interactions, and aspirations. Your Sun career line indicates power places where you tend to gain the most public recognition, and is where you want to be to leverage your potential and upscale your innate strengths.

When your Sun career line is activated, you'll be more inclined to assume positions of authority. Power places along this line are not for exploring new careers where you have little expertise, but are where you want to rise and peak in your professional life, like the Sun at noon. It's the line for those seeking recognition and validation through entrepreneurship, management, leadership roles, or becoming the most cited academic in your field.

TAKE THE LEAD

Expect to thrive in leadership roles on your Sun line. This can mean guiding a team, running a business, or influencing others. While some lines may enliven supporting roles, your Sun power places for career invite attention and prestige, but also scrutiny.

FEEL THE MOTIVATION

Expect to feel empowered and self-motivated in your career on the Sun line. We all know those jobs where we wake up with a sense of dread for the day. But not on the Sun line, which tends to boost energy and self-directed purpose.

BEWARE OF PRESSURE

The danger on the Sun career line is putting too much pressure on yourself to perform. If you're already high-achieving and a perfectionistic, the Sun line can amplify these tendencies. But sometimes, you have to pay the cost to be the boss.

EXPECT THANKS

When you combine energy, confidence, and self-motivation on your Sun career line, expect recognition for your work. Whether it's in corporate life or public-facing roles, this is where you'll be seen and appreciated, rather than neglected in your cubicle despite the 80-hour weeks.

CAREERS SUPPORTED BY THE SUN

MENTORSHIP	Motivational speaker or leadership coach are two career paths that empower others, while also letting your leadership capabilities shine.
FITNESS & WELLNESS	Think fitness trainer, wellness coach, or even public health administration, all of which bring people to greater vitality.
ARTS & ENTERTAINMENT	Acting, directing, newscasting, and influencing are all roles that put you at the centre of the public eye.
START-UPS	Consider pursuing your own startup company (big or small) to provide best-in-class solutions for your entrepreneurial spirit, and be your own boss.

The Sun

Home Line

The Sun home line tends to reflect your personality and patterns more than others, because the Sun represents demonstrative energy. This means this line can sometimes feel like a stage – full of fun and comedy, but also some drama. Accordingly, power places on the Sun home line might seem a bit like a dramedy, as you might tend to perform more at social gatherings, around the hearth, or at family dinners.

Additionally, on your Sun home line, you may be more drawn to spotlight your achievements, passions, and ancestry. Remember, the Sun line has to do with showing and about making yourself visible and shining. Don't be surprised if your employee of the month plaque from a decade ago finds pride of place near the TV for all to see.

GO BOLD

Expect a home brimming with creativity and bold design choices, perhaps with a hint of theatricality, as Sun energy speaks to a flair for the dramatic. You may also be drawn to bright tones more than usual.

SHOWCASE FAMILY

While you may not want to design your own family crest (although that's the sort of flair for the dramatic that life on the Sun line is all about), showcase your family history and your own achievements when on this powerful line.

BUILD YOUR LEGACY

Expect your desire to build a legacy for your family to become more pronounced on your Sun home line. This legacy may be inspired by a focus on your ancestry, or an intensified desire for securing a future for your family via material comforts and financial security due.

> The Sun home line tends to reflect your personality and patterns more than others, because the Sun represents demonstrative energy.

THE
MOON

Intuition | Emotion
Nurture | Fertility | Home Life

Your Moon line points to power places where you may experience a deeper emotional connection to the world around you, as well as clearer insight into your feelings about work, relationships, and home. Those living on or visiting their Moon line tend to nurture emotional bonds, engage in healing and self-care, and reconnect with the past. While it may cause you to feel more vulnerable or sensitive, the Moon line ultimately encourages emotional wellbeing and security.

The Planet of Feelings

In contrast to the Sun, which functions like a spotlight as we step onto the world's stage, we can think of the Moon as a kind of candlelight by which we read our lines in private. Because of its association with privacy, interiority, and feeling, the Moon often gets linked to the archetype of the Mother. While this gendering of the cosmos has become somewhat outmoded, the Moon can help us feel emotionally whole, nurtured, or safe. It can also help align with who we really are, and answer questions like: what is really motivating me? Why am I performing this role? And how do I feel about it?

The Moon's Light Qualities

When you are connected to the light energies of the Moon, your emotional energy will express itself in nurturing, empathetic, and supportive ways. You may have an innate ability to care for others, and when aligned with the Moon, you are more likely to be secure within yourself. This internal emotional security can give you the strength to offer genuine compassion to others.

The Moon's Shadow Qualities

The dark side of the Moon is that it can expose some of the more challenging aspects of your emotional world, like heightened reactivity, coldness, or erratic mood swings. Rather than expressing nurture and care, the Moon's shadow side can manifest as defensiveness, where you may feel the need to protect yourself from perceived threats or emotional harm, or act with excessive emotional investment or possessiveness.

Life on the Moon Line

Safe. Secure. Spiritually sound. Those who live on or travel to their Moon line tend to characterize it as an experience of increased emotional sensitivity, where they feel more connected with their feelings, instincts, and surroundings. This heightened emotional awareness tends to make power places on your Moon line particularly fecund sites to start or grow a family, reconnect with loved ones, or settle down to the world of domestic comforts.

This line is particularly good for those who are done with nightlife and its smoke-machine charades, or who need to restore themselves after decades of depleted conversations in the Kafkaesque corridors of corporate life. It is also a powerful place for those who seek alignment with their ancestry or the history of a place.

Ultimately, living on or visiting your Moon line suggests places for nurturing yourself and your loved ones, as by connecting with the Moon's energy, you can enliven more emotional security and a sense of belonging into your life.

TRAVELLING ON
YOUR MOON LINE

BEST FOR
family trips; nurturing relationships; introspective calm; self-care; emotional healing and growth; deepening relationships; or reconnecting with loved ones.

WHAT TO PLAN
mindful walks through serene gardens; moments of quiet reflection; journalling; self-care; or simply allowing your emotions to unfold naturally.

WHAT TO PACK
a sleeping mask; lavender essential oil; a silver dream journal; comfortable clothing; mediation tools like a portable cushion or yoga mat; a copy of Sigmund Freud's *The Interpretation of Dreams* to enrich your journey with a deeper understanding of your subconscious and emotional landscape.

The Moon

AC ——————— Personal Line

The Moon personal line speaks to where you can more freely express your caring nature, inner child, or emotional truths. Where the Moon home line points to family and building community around the hearth, the Moon personal line is for your own growth. It's about healing yourself, but not through a romantic partner or family. This is the line for self-care.

This doesn't mean you'll be alone on this line. Rather, this line is for those wanting to develop their capacity for emotional intelligence by first looking at themselves, or for those seeking to break out of bad emotional patterns in the name of becoming a more fully realized bearer of light, hope, and change.

GROW YOUR EMOTIONAL IQ

Expect to make strides in understanding your emotional
needs and those of others. While understanding doesn't
necessarily mean clarity, as your emotional IQ grows,
you'll develop the ability to navigate emotional complexity
with greater nuance and depth.

TRUST YOUR BASIC INSTINCTS

By enlivening your connection to your emotional
landscape, the Moon personal line invites you to
act on your intuition more. Whether it's in decisions
about relationships, career moves, or personal
growth, expect your instincts to guide you.

LISTEN TO YOUR INNER CHILD

This line is a site for personal healing, so
expect to hear the voice of your inner child
more. Listen to their complaints, but then work
to put them to bed. Emotional balance is key.

TAKE A SPA YEAR

We often talk about spa days, but consider
travel or longer stays on your Moon personal
line as an extended opportunity to nurture
yourself. Sometimes a spa day isn't enough.
This line may also be used for bigger
self-restoration projects like recovering
from an illness, accident, or broken heart.

The Moon

DC ————— ## Relationship Line

The Moon relationship line pushes us to get past any fears or vulnerabilities that we are scared to share or confront, not just with ourselves, but with a partner. By enlivening Moon energy, power places on this line tend to attract people to us who are ready for emotional honesty and openness. That doesn't mean that things will be smooth sailing, but they will at least be real.

Relationships on the Moon relationship line incline towards emotional processing, talking, opening up, and exploration. Your relationships on this line need not be strictly romantic; any deep one-on-one scenario (say, with a business partner) should become more open and free on this line, which is ultimately for those needing reciprocity, understanding, and acceptance.

SEEK DEPTH, NOT SURFACES

Allow people to see the real you, even if that can be a bit messy. Indeed, the deeper we dig, the muddier things get. But there's nothing wrong with getting somewhat dirty; learning that is the first step to real intimacy.

LOOK FOR MIRRORS, NOT WALLS

Rather than relationships that feel like you're banging your head against a wall, the Moon relationship line attracts mirroring relationships that show you sides and angles of yourself that you may have never seen before. And vice versa.

EMBRACE THE COUCH

Expect to find someone who provides a safe emotional and physical space. Forget clubs; the couch will be your hot destination. This isn't to say you won't have any fun, but this isn't the line for wild nights and wild partners.

EXPECT HEALING, NOT HEADACHES

We are all cracked, broken, dented, or scratched up in some way (it's sad, but true). But expect Moon relationships to help heal these bumps and bruises. Partnerships should feel more like a balm than a bad burn.

The Moon

MC ———— Career Line

Salvador Dalí, famous for his surrealist art, had his Moon career line running through Paris. And it was in Paris that he met André Breton, the founder of Surrealism, and, under the influence of this dreamlike art form, created his most famous pieces, such as *The Persistence of Memory* with its indelible melting clocks.

Dalí serves as an example of how a career on your Moon line is about finding professional fulfilment by contacting your innermost impulses. This line is not for working on projects that feel distant from your core values, fascinations, or feelings. Instead, it's for enlivening career opportunities that dovetail with causes you care deeply about, or connecting with projects for which you've had longstanding, heartfelt fascinations.

GET IN WHERE YOU FIT IN

So much of professional life is about fitting in where you get in with a job, but you can reverse that trend on your Moon career line by engaging in work that feels like you're with family or friends.

CHOOSE YOUR HEART OVER YOUR HEAD

This line draws you towards careers that feel emotionally fulfilling, and guides you towards work that nourishes you and helps you nourish others. Instead of overanalysing a job offer, trust your gut feelings.

REDEFINE SUCCESS

Careers on this line aren't about bright lights and social status
in the way that those on your Sun career line might be. Success
on the Moon career line is more about internal reward, so define
your success by how your career makes you feel at the end of
the day, and how it makes others feel.

EMPATIZE AND LISTEN

Leave any swaggering CEO mentality behind and lean into
softer leadership skills where you learn to listen not just to
others you work with, but to your own feelings too.

CAREERS SUPPORTED BY THE MOON

THERAPY	The Moon's propensity to make us better at listening makes careers in therapy and counselling auspicious.
FOOD & HOSPITALITY	Cooking and food-related careers such as being a chef, baker, or barista allow you to nourish others.
INTERIOR DESIGN OR HOMEMAKING	Designing or maintaining spaces that provide comfort and emotional security for others embodies quintessential Moon energy.
CAREGIVING	Nursing, midwifery, childminding, and caregiving are perfect for those who want to physically and emotionally nurture others.

The Moon

IC ——— Home Line

The Moon home line is where you might be drawn to establish meaningful traditions and rituals with yourself and those closest to you. Of all the home lines on your star map, this one is the most quintessentially homelike.

My Moon home line runs through Chicago (my favourite spot in America, if not the world), and the first time I ever visited and looked out at Lake Michigan in its wintry indifference, I felt oddly at peace. Now, I try to make it back there at least once a year, and, during my returns, I've developed my own traditions that make Chicago feel like home to me. When you activate this line, it's the little things you do that make you feel comfortable in the world.

EMBRACE CREATURE COMFORTS

This line is all about getting cosy, so try to incorporate features in your home that align with Moon energy, like plants, soft colour palettes, low wattage lighting (like the moonlight itself), and large communal spaces for family. Overall, a lunar home should feel soft and traditional, not sleek and modern.

FLY THE NEST SOMETIMES

This line provides the ultimate nesting energy,
but you still need to get out, have fun, and explore
other power places on your star map. Try not to let
the comfort of the Moon home line turn into what
John Milton called "ignoble ease". Home is great,
but getting away from it is good for you too.

SEEK PEACE AND QUIET

Even if your Moon home line runs through busy cities,
you want your space to feel peaceful and quiet, and to be
a site for reflection, security, and feeling calm. This could
mean anything from finding a lovely apartment on an
adorable side street to matching with a lunar roommate
who is kind, clean, and considerate.

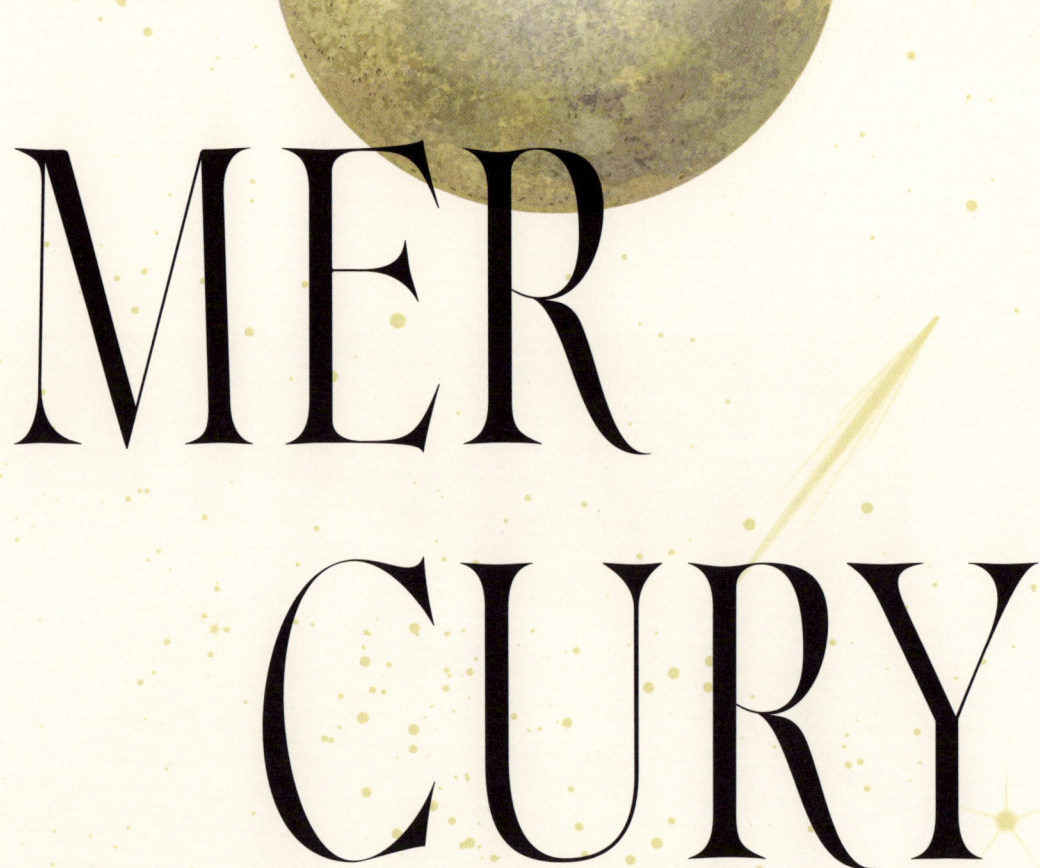

MER CURY

Self-Expression | Intellect
Networking | Freneticism

The Mercury line highlights power places where communication, learning, and business acumen are heightened, along with an intensified curiosity about the world. Those who activate their Mercury line, either through travel, remote access, or relocation, tend to enjoy increased opportunities, especially in areas related to writing and education. Although it can lead to overly frenetic mental activity, the Mercury line indicates places excellent for self-expression, as well as robust social interaction.

The Messenger Planet

Associated with intellect, wit, and analytical acumen, Mercury is the smart one in astrology.

As a cosmic principle, Mercury governs communications and commerce. Etymologically, the Latin verb mercari meant "to trade", and the classical mythology surrounding Mercury also touches upon these qualities. In Roman myth, Mercury is the god of travelers, thieves, and tricksters. In Greek myth, Mercury (known as the god Hermes) transited between the worlds of the dead, the divine, and the human, gathering intel on and dispensing messages to all three. As such, Hermes was known as the Messenger, and so, in its astrological context, Mercury also impacts expression and communication.

Mercury's Light Qualities

Mercury in its light side can be quick-witted, clever, dynamic, and versatile. It can also be sociable and persuasive, filled with curiosity and a love of knowledge. Mercury in a birth chart might exhibit brilliant rhetorical skill, or a focus on strategizing on how best to bring about the public good.

Mercury's Shadow Qualities

The shadow side to Mercury might express itself in a birth chart through duplicitous speech, excessive nosiness, freneticism, irritability, caprice, and fussiness, which is to say, being too precise and analytical. Furthermore, while Mercury is associated with commerce (the trading of goods), it is also linked with thievery (the stealing of them) and trickery.

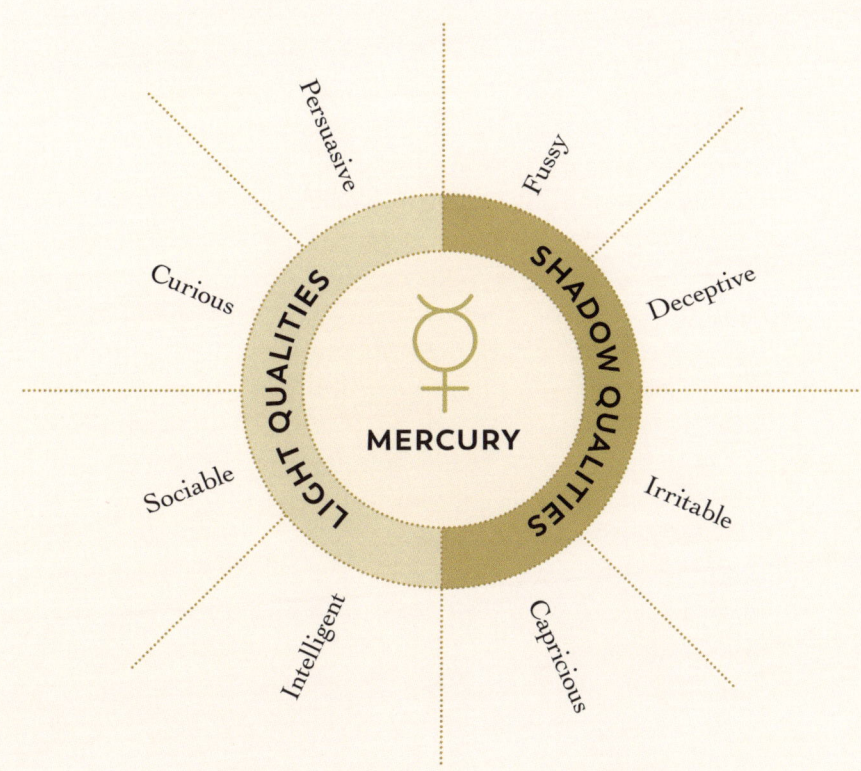

Life on the Mercury Line

Fast, not slow. Busy, not still. People who travel or relocate to their Mercury power places are seeking stimulation in some way. This is not a line for repose, recovery, or relaxation. Instead, Mercury power places tend to intensify mental activity, emphasizing the pleasure of doing business, intellectual pursuits, and deep dynamic communication between friends, partners, or colleagues.

On the Mercury line, you might discover your inner poet or excel in professions that rely heavily on rhetorical skills. Relationships may brim with enthusiasm over brunch as you and a partner's conversations provide more caffeine than the coffee. Similarly, home life on the Mercury line will tend to be dynamic, fun, and maybe even a bit hectic.

Those looking to be adaptable in business, life, and love will find inspiration here, as you find yourself always in motion and ever-curious about your surroundings. The caveat in all this though is that the Mercury line can make you restless and mentally frenetic, as you jet through your days, multitasking and negotiating. But, to alter Tennyson a bit, "Tis better to have moved and lost, than to never have moved at all." If that's how you feel, then your Mercury line is worth checking out in more detail.

**TRAVELLING ON
YOUR MERCURY LINE**

BEST FOR
brainstorming weekends;
boosting productivity; overcoming
shyness and writer's block; crafting
a book or blog; networking; a coding
bootcamp; staying up late; perusing
curiosity shops and record stores;
or thriving in fast-paced
environments.

**WHAT
TO PLAN**
activities to keep your
mind sharp; conversations
with strangers; or visits to
byzantine streets, cities,
or ports that see masses
of people about their
daily hustle.

**WHAT
TO PACK**
your laptop; a notebook; a
camera; earphones for moments
when you need to focus; many
changes of multicoloured clothes; and
Samuel Delany's *Trouble on Triton*, a novel
with Afrofuturist and genderqueer
resonances that explores the
high-speed, cybernetic
nature of city-space and
identity-in-flux.

The Mercury
AC ——————— Personal Line

The Mercury personal line is all about self-development, but with Mercury's energy involved, such personal progress will tend to come through little things, like mastering a very specific topic through study or learning a new skill. Satisfaction will be achieved through specialized domains of knowledge and experience rather than grandiose plans. The microscope, rather than the telescope, will be your technology for self-improvement.

Mercury's association with intellect may also prompt you to identify more as an intellectual on this line, as you develop talents for thinking deeply about topics and expressing them to others through the written word. Being seen for your mind, rather than your heart, may be a guiding motivation here.

PRACTISE MENTAL GYMNASTICS

This line will sharpen your mental agility, so is the place
to generate ideas for your next big art project, script, novel,
essay, or documentary, as you absorb and inquire into the
culture around you.

ACQUIRE LANGUAGE

There are no better places than those on your Mercury
relationship line to learn a second, third, or fourth
language. Computer coding and other such systems
may be more easily learned here too.

BEWARE OF ATTENTION DEFICIT

One downside to Mercury is being too curious
about things to the detriment of sustained focus.
Be careful not to lose yourself in things, rather
than finding yourself in them.

BE A SOCIAL BUTTERFLY

Network like a pro to develop yourself, not
your career ambitions. Seek others who
give you insider knowledge on where the
best yoga studios, ashrams, church
services, or synagogues are located.

The Mercury

DC ———— Relationship Line

This line tends to be powerful for attracting intellectually dazzling types to you, or for you to be more attracted to these types than you would be elsewhere. You may be drawn to someone's mind rather than physical beauty, as repartee, wit, and intellectual conversations provide their own sexual currency.

Because knowledge and intellect become important on this line, you may also be drawn to romantic situations where you play a willingly subordinate role to someone of letters and intellectual prestige. And, since Mercury's energy is adaptable, you may also shift your opinions or thinking on certain topics like politics, as you deepen your intellectual journey on your Mercury relationship line.

BE STIMULATED

On this line, relationships are built on conversation and the pleasures of listening. Expect mentally stimulating partnerships where dialogue and exchanging ideas are central. You'll be particularly drawn to partners who challenge your intellect and pique your curiosity.

GO LIGHT, NOT HEAVY

The people you meet on this line will bring a sense of joy and spontaneity, avoiding the heavy, melodramatic tones that can weigh down romance. Embrace the fun and carefree energy, allowing relationships to flourish without unnecessary burdens.

FEEL YOUNG AND RESTLESS

One thing to beware of on this line is that while relationships may feel exciting and dynamic, they may sometimes struggle with emotional depth. Mercury energy tends to attract youthfulness or its spirit into your life, so power places on this line may exhibit the thrills, but also the shallowness and restlessness of youth.

FIND CREATIVE SOLUTIONS

Partnerships on this line are excellent for problem-solving and finding compromises. Both you and your partner will likely have a quick-thinking, solution-oriented approach to any challenges in the relationship.

The Mercury
MC ———————— Career Line

I have a French client whose Mercury career line crosses through Copenhagen, where she works in the dizzying world of fashion PR. She is constantly hustling, publicizing, socializing, and coaxing media outlets to talk about clients, and clients to talk about products in a careful choreography of flattery, snark, and sass. She works crazy hours. She sleeps little. She is often frazzled when we speak. But, most importantly, she loves what she does.

This is classic Mercury career line stuff, where your professional life becomes supercharged. Here, opportunities may come from networking or connecting with influential figures who recognize your Mercury-sharpened mind, which is always curious for new information and skills. This might also be a place where where you make a name for yourself, or where your voice is heard, especially through speaking engagements, social media, or writing. Ultimately, this line is for hustlers (or for those who want to hustle more).

LEND A HELPING HAND
The Mercury career line isn't about being the CEO, but rather the facilitator who knows all the backdoor angles to execute the vision of leadership. Aim to be more like the hand of the ruler whose logistical brilliance creates professional connections, synergies, and profits.

DON'T FORGET TO REST

Though the career benefits are significant, one potential downside to working on this line is the mental stimulation that comes with it. The need to stay mentally sharp can lead to overwork, restlessness, or burnout if you're not careful, so it's important to balance the high-speed, intellectually demanding environment with rest to avoid mental exhaustion.

EMBRACE SMOOTHER TALKING

On this line, expect smooth negotiation skills that mint multi-billion-dollar deals (or at least help you hit your monthly commission target). There is a charisma that gets enhanced on your Mercury career line where effortless engagement with clients in conversation puts them at ease, while exuding expertise.

CAREERS SUPPORTED BY MERCURY

WRITING & JOURNALISM	Whether you are crafting novels, penning articles, or creating content for digital platforms, your ability to articulate ideas will be at its peak here.
LOGISTICS	M stands for Mercury and mobility, so careers coordinating the movement of goods or services is highly supported.
PR & MARKETING	These fields require excellent communication skills and the ability to craft compelling messages.
SALES & NEGOTIATION	Success in sales and negotiation relies heavily on persuasive communication. Power places on the Mercury line will support careers that mobilize this skillset.

The Mercury
IC ———— Home Line

The Mercury home line propends towards an environment that may be quite busy. Here, you may be prone to bringing work home, or your home office space may extend into the living space proper. Rather than Scandinavian calm, life on this line will be filled with small things like curios, knickknacks, and mementos.

In terms of family dynamics, the Mercury home line activates vibrant communication, establishing an environment where you will tend to talk things through rather than talk over or at each other. Debate, discussion, and dialogue dominate this line rather than dysfunction, which may make this line feel like a social hub for the neighbourhood community. Loneliness and solitude will tend not to be an option.

CREATE A SMART HOME

Intellectual debate will tend to be the tenor of conversation here, as well as the spirit of intellectual inquiry. Expect to find yourself more inclined towards technological integration – like gamified learning apps or virtual learning platforms – to enhance learning and communication for your family, especially children.

BE HELPFUL

Mercury inspires us to get things done for others, so focus on anticipating the needs of family and helping them fulfil them as you demonstrate exquisite care, attention to detail, and curiosity about the lives of those around you.

MAKE (RE)ARRANGEMENTS

Life on this line means embracing Mercury's mutable and mobile spirit, so you may find yourself drawn to rearrange your space or switch up your living situation, driven by need for change.

The Mercury home line propends towards an environment that may be quite busy.

VENUS

Beauty | Relationships | Creativity
Love | Harmony | Luxury

The Venus line charts power places where romance thrives. Those living on or visiting hotspots along their Venus line tend to speak of enhanced charm and attractiveness in social situations, increased success in relationships, and intensified creativity (especially around music and the arts). While it may make you more prone to luxurious expenditure and pleasure-seeking, the Venus line ultimately maps locations that heighten self-esteem, foster a harmonious living environment, and provide more opportunities for love.

The Planet of Love

Venus, associated with desire and romance helps delineate the rules of attraction. It sprinkles fairy dust on some people and broadens the shoulders of others to allow for social harmony and cohesion. Venus functions as a kind of cosmic glue whose essence is to help people come together, and teach us: how do we give love? How do we receive it? Why is this beloved so sweet? This one so sour? Why are we romantically drawn to this person, but not that one?

Venus's Light Qualities

Venus's light qualities bring love, melody, and harmony into our life, elevating our sensibility through the power of beauty. As such, it also brings pleasure (both giving it and receiving it) through amorous interactions or creative pursuits. Venus's light energy can also energize things like charisma with co-workers, as well as harmony between them.

Venus's Shadow Qualities

The flipside to this planet is idleness and excessive pleasure seeking to the detriment of honest labour, discipline, and the character-building that comes from both. It can also cause us to become too entangled in love, taking focus away from all other areas of life except for relationships.

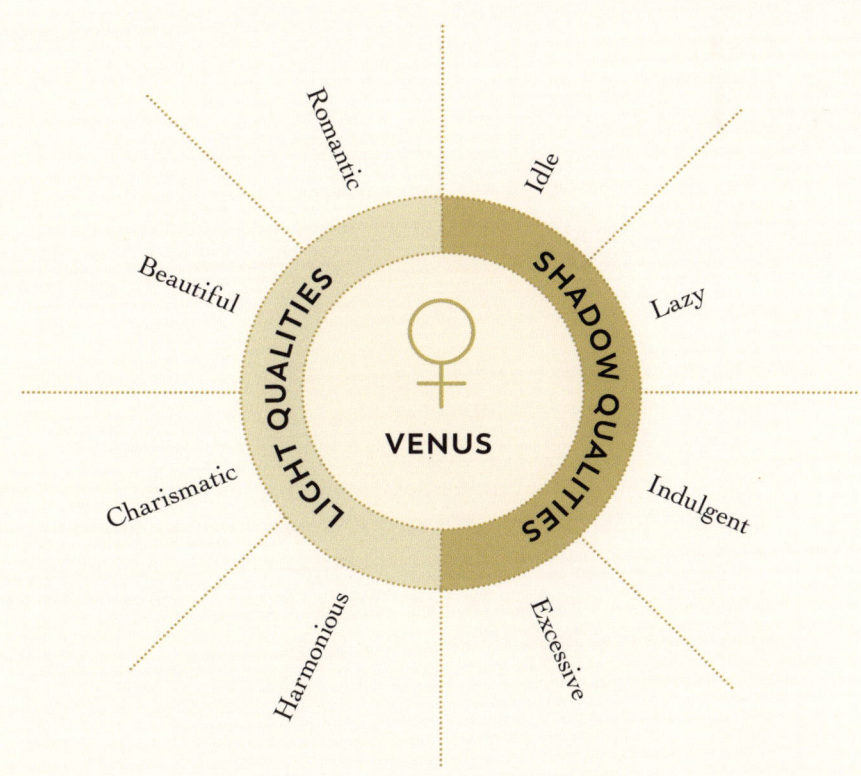

Life on the Venus Line

Romance. Love. Flourishing relationships. These are the typical motivations for relocating or visiting the Venus line, and while these are indeed powerful reasons, you shouldn't limit the way you think about the influence of Venus in your life to just love.

Indeed, Venusian power places may also enliven your artistic talents, as Venus is about creativity too. To give a great example, one of Michelangelo's Venus lines crossed through Rome, the place where he blessed us with his timeless masterpiece in the Vatican's Sistine Chapel.

But, in the words of John Lennon, "Love is all you need", and you can't get more Venusian than that. To use John as a further example, his Venus line ran through Japan, the birthplace of his wife Yoko, while Yoko's crossed through John's hometown in England, and both were advocates for peace and a world of no conflict or borders.

This reference to peace and no conflict can further sum up the energies to be found on the Venus line, as Venus wants to make your life easy. The struggle or discipline you may find on other lines like Saturn or Pluto tend not to manifest in Venusian power places, as ease reigns supreme here, making it a beneficial line to work with in all areas of life.

TRAVELLING ON YOUR VENUS LINE

BEST FOR

coquettish behaviour; embracing romance and beauty; boosting self-esteem; navigating a breakup; reigniting confidence; shopping sprees to revitalize your wardrobe; flirting; meeting charming individuals; or immersing yourself in beautiful surroundings.

WHAT TO PLAN

romantic strolls in idyllic places; visits to art galleries and places of beauty; fancy hotels; sumptuous restaurants; or erotic places.

WHAT TO PACK

items that amplify your sense of beauty, luxury, and eroticism; risqué lingerie; all your bling; a comfortable robe and slippers; rose pink clothes; and Marcel Proust's *In Search of Lost Time*, the greatest novel on love and Paris ever penned.

The Venus
AC — Personal Line

Power places on this line will show a path towards developing as a person through self-acceptance, as this line is all about providing a safe space to grow. Rather than being too hard, it encourages you to be soft and invites you to go easy on yourself.

The Venus personal line is a place where you can travel or relocate to avoid the self-recrimination that could arise from a traumatic event in your life or a relationship that did more harm than good. This is also a line where you can work to be fair-minded to yourself and others, as you look to exhibit forgiveness rather than tough love.

On a more superficial level, this line may also refer to personal development by refining your physical appearance. Cosmetic surgery, lux retreats, or other beautifying regimes will all be supported here.

BOOST YOUR SELF-WORTH
On this line, you'll feel drawn to the luxury of self-appreciation, as if you're the high-end piece in the window display of your soul. Work with this line to recognize that you're something worth investing in.

GIVE PEACE A CHANCE
Try to put less pressure on yourself to perform and excel on this line, as this will make it easier to navigate relationships and develop a supportive environment around you.

EMBRACE GRACE

We all know that feeling of being uncomfortable in our own skin, but on this line, expect to feel more at ease with yourself. Venus has a tendency to endow our appearance and movement through the world with grace rather than gawkiness.

LET ART IMITATE LIFE

This is a line not only to make yourself feel pretty on the inside and outside, but to develop your creative talents by making beautiful objects, too. Venus is ultimately about creating beauty in the world, so embrace your artistic side, and don't be afraid to share your work with others.

The Venus
DC ——— Relationship Line

Venus and relationships go together like coffee and cream, and power places on this line suggest hotspots to get married or find a partner you might eventually tie the knot with. This is where you may feel more attractive to others, lighting up rooms with charm and grace. There's something of a Cinderella-like magic on this line, without the overly punitive midnight curfew.

Relationships on the Venus line will tend to be suffused with pleasure and indulgence. This is the perfect line for finding a new romance that is about easy and fun connection. By the same token, if you are currently in a somewhat difficult, though ultimately loving relationship, vacations to power places on this line can help bring some much needed sweetness, as you re-enliven the joys of disporting in the boudoir, eye-gazing, and hand-holding.

MASTER THE ART OF COMPROMISE

Expect a knack for compromise and finding the middle ground in relationships on this line. You and your partner will be better at taking each other's needs into account when making decisions. Approach disagreements gently, seeking solutions that satisfy both parties.

BEWARE OF TOO MUCH CHILL

On this line, beware of too much pleasure-seeking with a partner. Venus energy loves to relax, pamper, spend, and party. Given this tendency, you need to be on the lookout for making the bedroom your headquarters. Balance and some restraint is necessary.

GO FOR STYLE AND SUBSTANCE

On this line, expect to attract relationships that others admire. You may be seen as part of a "power couple", which will add extra gloss to your Venusian self-esteem. But the concern here is that image will become everything. Work on the inner beauty of a relationship, too, through compromise and multilateralism.

The Venus Career Line

MC ——————

Careers on the Venus line tend to go smoothly and without much effort. Instead of strenuous or emotionally-taxing labour, this line may provide opportunities that feel light, fun, and sweet. Consider this line if you need a break from the heavy grind or want to pursue something a bit lighter career-wise.

Careers on this line may also be inclined towards the beauty industry, the arts, or professions that bring people together in some harmonious way. Even though image isn't necessarily everything, Venus is the planet of beauty, so careers on this line could have you feeling more conscious of appearances, whether that means stepping up your fashion game due to a career opportunity, or fashioning looks and styles for others.

PRIORITIZE LIFE

On some lines, work dominates, but on the Venus line, enjoying life does. Seek career opportunities that allow you time to pursue side-projects or your passions, as Venus energy is about pleasure.

PLAY WELL WITH OTHERS

Venus is the great harmonizer, so develop your tact, negotiation, and conflict resolution skills. On this line, be able to mediate and collaborate better, thereby establishing healthier professional environments.

BE APPROACHABLE

Venus energy attracts people to us. In a professional context, this means being approachable in the form of an easy, charming demeanour. Embody this energy and expect more networking opportunities and clients to arise as a consequence.

ENJOY MATERIAL COMFORTS

Venus is about harmony, but it's also about cash, luxury, and material goods. Don't be ashamed to be driven by material comforts and a desire for tangible results on this line, whether it's in the form of financial rewards, completed projects, or well-crafted products.

CAREERS SUPPORTED BY VENUS

BRAND STRATEGY	Venus energy is image-oriented, making it ideal for careers that focus on cultivating brand identity, logo design, and advertising strategy.
EVENT PLANNING	Bringing people together in the spirit of joy and celebration aligns perfectly with Venus energy, whether it's organizing weddings or corporate gatherings.
BEAUTY	Any career related to personal care, cosmetics, skincare, haircare, fragrance, and overall aesthetics aligns with this line.
MEDIATION	Venus influences us and others to avoid conflicts, making mediation between individuals or groups to resolve disputes an auspicious career choice.

The Venus

IC —————— # Home Line

On this line, you may be more prone to display art or beautiful objects. You may also be inspired to beautify your home through renovations that utilize the space in unique ways. Because Venusian energy intensifies fertility, these places may be ripe spaces for creating and maintaining gardens as a source of pleasure, nourishment, and harmonizing with the natural world.

While the Venus home naturally indicates a place for love, balance, and refinement in a social as well as domestic sense, one challenge on this line may be that your family may shy away from tougher conversations for the sake of equilibrium. Ultimately, the Venus home line fosters joy and beauty in the simple pleasures of a well-loved home with harmony at its foundation.

BE FINANCIALLY SAVVY

Venus energy can be all about luxury, but it's also an expert negotiator. Expect to find good fortune and good value with real estate or inheritances on this line.

BE A DOMESTIC JUSTICE WARRIOR

Family life is not to be ruled by an iron-fist on this line, but by the deft touch of fairness and consensus arrived at through peaceful and mature discussion.

SEEK LUX SOPHISTICATION

Embrace Venusian things in your home like tasteful artwork, proportional furniture, and subtle and sophisticated colour palettes. Opt for a home that feels pleasing with a hint of lux, rather than overflowing and maximalist.

TAKE A STROLL

Imagine sisters in a Jane Austen novel, sitting in hushed elegance, talking about books and boys, then taking a stroll about the manor's trim gardens under parasols so as not to get too much Sun. Disruptions minimal, very Venus. Emulate this.

MARS

Action | Drive | Passion
Growth Through Conflict

The Mars line maps power places that enliven your passions, drive for greatness, and will to compete. Those who live on or visit their Mars line may experience intensified focus around career and the need for honours and rewards. A desire for increased physical activity and sports training could also manifest. While the Mars line may bring challenges in the form of confrontational behaviour, it ultimately indicates locations where you might go to push yourself to the limit in the name of personal growth.

The Planet of Action

Mars is often called the "Minor Malefic" and "the Planet of War", as it is traditionally seen as an energy that repels. However, Mars is also known to have warrior energy, which can manifest in valour and loyalty to greater causes and codes of conduct. It can influence us to fight against injustice, and to fight for ideas, people, places, and things we value. At its best, Mars can provide our lives with the raw energy to get stuff done, as well as the courage to battle for the stuff we believe in.

Mars's Light Qualities

In its light side, Mars functions as a kind of cosmic motor that drives us forwards, inducing us to action and decision-making. While these decisions might be rash, they at least get made. Mars shoots first and asks questions later, and sometimes we need this in our lives. This energy can also be incredibly beneficial for a sensitive personality that has trouble asserting themselves, for example, when asking for a raise or promotion.

Mars's Shadow Qualities

In its shadow side, Mars can be reckless and brutal, and can manifest in rude or gruff speech and uncouth actions. Here, Mars's warlike energy can have negative effects that manifest as too much aggression and competitiveness. Where the positives of Mars may encourage someone to ask for a raise after a decade of quiet hard work, the darker side of Mars might cause someone to alienate everyone in their attempt to plant their red flag atop the proverbial hill of VP of Sales.

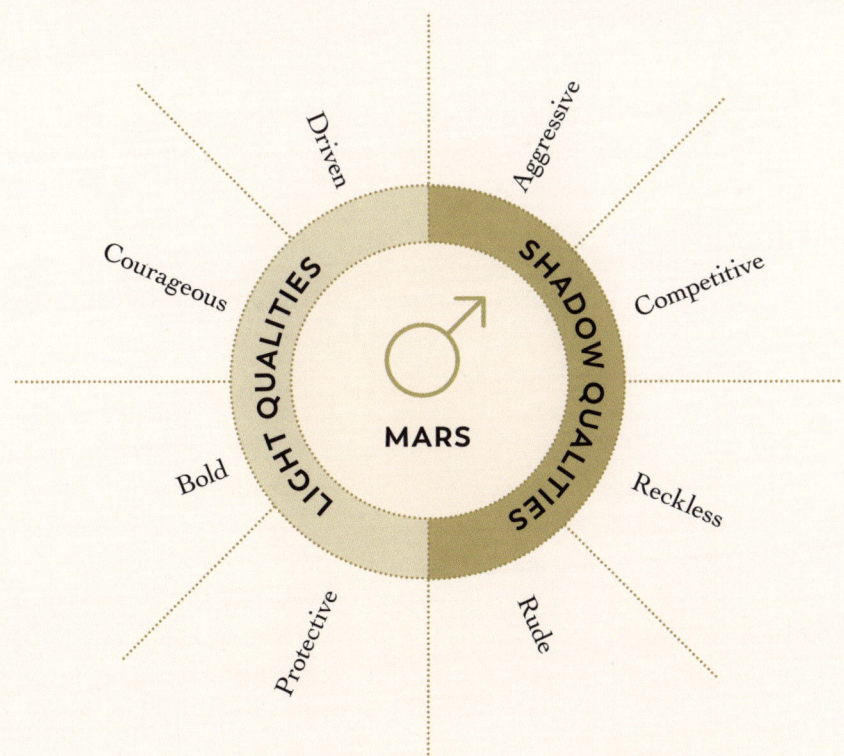

Life on the Mars Line

Hot. Energetic. Driven. I often tell my clients that Mars power places are highly caffeinated places that you go to when you want to wake up and get moving with your life.

The Mars line suggests locations to go to if you're ready to compete with others. These are not hotspots for teamwork; life here resembles a battlefield where endurance, assertiveness, and strength are cosmically enhanced. If you're doubting yourself or needing to prove something to someone, this is the line you go to.

This is a great line for training or testing yourself with some sporty goal in mind. Getting in shape, becoming ultra-health conscious, and preparing for a gruelling triathlon are the kinds of activities associated with Mars power places. Or, it could be a place where you visit to up your sex drive.

Going to your Mars line is akin to bringing a Mars transit to you. Things get accelerated fast, and you become bolder than you ever thought possible. Mars's influence can be, in certain contexts, aggressive. But in others it can lend us the energy and bravery we need to take on a huge passion project, try a change in career, or ask out the bartender who seems bookish and down-to-earth.

TRAVELLING ON YOUR MARS LINE

BEST FOR
addressing issues head on; standing up for yourself; being assertive; adventure and physical challenges; being bold; getting in shape; or intense training.

WHAT TO PLAN
running a marathon; skydiving; bungee jumping; hiking rugged trails; testing your endurance; extreme sports; activities that encourage you to embrace your fearless side; or sports weekends to see your team play.

WHAT TO PACK
sneakers; workout clothes; windbreakers; red items to enliven the energy of Mars; protein bars and other nutritional supplements to keep you shredded; and biographies about CEOs and other titans of industry who crushed their competition.

The Mars
AC —————— Personal Line

As a planet, Mars indicates our most self-assertive and self-centred energy, so the Mars personal line is for those who are not looking to get into family mode, play the dating game, or really move forward with their career. Rather, it's where you go to strengthen your character, your resolve, or your sense of personal power in order to kickstart a career, romance, or family. If you are feeling rudderless, this line provides the motive force to establish routines and practices of self-improvement to find yourself.

Think of this line as basic training where you enter somewhat out-of-shape and scattered, but emerge in a crisp uniform, with perfect posture, with the newfound inner intensity of a cadet.

PRACTISE SELF-DISCIPLINE
Always remember, warlike Mars indicates militaristic energy. Use this energy to promote focus and determination as they relate to personal goals around fitness, career, or personal projects. This is a line for getting your life back on track if you've let yourself go, or for taking your life to a new level of high-intensity training.

BE ASSERTIVE
If you have trouble setting boundaries or vacillating on decisions, this line provides bold direction. It may make you somewhat reckless at times, but living here affects a sense of empowerment or forward motion at high speed.

GO SOLO
Embrace going at projects alone. While other lines may increase your desire for teamwork, coupledom, or the support of your friend network, this line is the equivalent of a solo hike into the wilderness accompanied only by a pulsing drive to reach that mountain peak by nightfall.

PRACTISE ANGER MANAGEMENT
Fiery Mars may bring up emotions like anger or frustration (especially towards ourselves) on this line, but try to channel that intensity into resilience. Expect to burn, but rise like a phoenix here.

The Mars
DC ——— Relationship Line

Power places on the Mars relationship line are where you might go when you want to focus on your career, but also enjoy the occasional comforts of intimacy with someone who is equally ambitious. You may live alone on this line or insist on keeping your apartment, even if you are in a steady relationship.

This isn't to say that the Mars relationship line is for non-commitment. Relationships on this line tend to be fiercely loyal ones all about passion and intensity, as the very distance that seems to create obstacles to intimacy is actually a precondition for it to thrive in relation to Mars. If you're looking for an autonomy that lets you breathe on your own terms, this line could be for you.

SPEAK UP

On this line, speak up and assert your needs with (blunt) clarity. Mars energy is not about sweet-talking. Communication should, therefore, be more direct and confident, even if this leads to conflict. This is a line where you can be fully honest with a partner and vice versa, but just remember that sometimes the truth hurts.

BEWARE OF COMBUSTIBILITY

Expect relationships on this line to be passionate and intense. Remember, Mars is all about fire. It tends to make us hot under the collar, and when you combine this combustibility, sparks will fly both at brunch and in the boudoir.

SHOW FIERCE LOYALTY

While Mars may influence you to get a bit too heated, it inspires loyalty to those you let into your life. Mars is a fighter. On this line, fight for your relationships as you protect their integrity.

The Mars

MC ———————— Career Line

The Mars career line suggests hotspots that enliven your ambition, thirst for power, and drive to do great things. Here, you'll feel inspired to overcome barriers in pursuit of your goals rather than get overwhelmed by them.

On this line, you may clash with authority figures. There is an almost adolescent sense of rebellion around Mars energy, which poses a bit of a problem for workplace politics. Because of this anti-authority streak, the Mars career line might be best for you if you're working to build your own brand, company, or social media presence. It's an excellent place for being your own boss and taking on the pressures that come from these kinds of riskier career paths, where everything depends on you.

GO BIG OR GO HOME
Fortune favours the bold, so in addition to self-assertion, expect to make some risky career decisions on this line. A go big or go home attitude will predominate over the safety of investing in government bonds with low annual yields.

FIND YOUR STAMINA

You should only align with Mars career power places when you're ready or willing to enter environments that require long hours, seemingly insurmountable tasks, and the difficulties that come with leadership. It's a hard road, but you may find strength you didn't know you had, making power places on this line ideal for impressing higher-ups on your career climb.

SHOW STRONG LEADERSHIP

Expect to command attention and be a great motivator on this line, while optimizing the performance of those you work around. A confident, clear communication style will tend to be enhanced here, so if you struggle with being bold, clear, and, at times, necessarily blunt, Mars energy can help with this.

CAREERS SUPPORTED BY MARS

ENTREPRENEURSHIP
Start-ups or passion projects that allow you to be in control of your own destiny, while taking big risks, is very Mars.

MILITARY & DEFENSE
Mars' association with combat means military careers such as soldier, officer, or defense contractor are a natural fit on this line.

ADVENTURE & OUTDOOR
Consider an outdoor guide or instructor, which allows you to lead others in adventurous Mars activities.

SPORTS & FITNESS
Careers such as personal trainer, coach, physical therapist, biomechanist, or athlete are perfect for this line.

The Mars

IC —————— # Home Line

Given the fierceness of Mars energy, you will likely find yourself functioning as a protector on this line more than others, and you may be more prone to maintaining proper boundaries with those in your home. This may mean regulating who comes and goes, including putting your foot down when it comes to in-laws overstaying a welcome or over-stepping proper decorum. The energy of this line may also manifest in standing up for family members within the community, even if that causes friction or bad blood in the neighbourhood.

In all this, remember the nature of Mars: it causes conflicts. There is no way around that energy. While tempers may flare between members of a household on this line, you can trust that this same energy will always be used to maintain the safety and protection of the home from enemies foreign, if not domestic.

BE ALONE, BUT TOGETHER

The great comedian Patrice O'Neal put it best when speaking about living with someone: "We want to be alone, but we don't want to be by ourselves." He must have lived on his Mars home line, since this perfectly characterizes its tenor. On this line, expect the desire for freedom and distance, but also the vague notion of familial togetherness.

EMBRACE COMPETITION

While autonomy is valued on this line, embrace the spirit of competition around the house when its denizens are together. Good-natured pasttimes (that can shift into fierce competitions in the backyard) will tend to energize family dynamics and serve as productive bonding mechanisms and tradition-builders.

DO IT YOURSELF

On this line, find the energy to carry out home-improvement yourself rather than going to licensed professionals. Such an impulse doesn't have to do with thriftiness, but rather self-sufficiency and self-reliance. Keep in mind, though, that Mars can be overly ambitious, so don't try to add an entire wing to the house. Just stick to more minor projects.

On the Mars home line, you may be more prone to maintaining proper boundaries with those in your home.

JUP ITER

Expansion | Opportunity
Luck | Excess | Spiritual Growth

The Jupiter line indicates power places where you might feel larger-than-life. Whether through remote access, travel, or a permanent relocation, those who engage with their Jupiter lines often experience increased optimism and benefit more from life's opportunities. Encouraging a journey towards greater knowledge and spiritual fulfilment, the Jupiter line brings about abundance in personal and professional development, although it can also push you towards excess in your behaviour and actions.

The Planet of Abundance

Astrologers call Jupiter our "Great Benefic", because its cosmic function in our lives is to maximise, enlarge, and expand. Nowhere is this greatness better expressed than in what is known as the Jupiter return, an astrological transit occurring every 12 years in someone's birth chart. Your Jupiter return marks the time when the planet returns to the same position in the sky as it was at your birth. During a Jupiter return, we receive more from the universe, life feels fuller, and we also are inspired to be more generous ourselves.

Jupiter Light Qualities

There is a holiness or spiritual quality to Jupiter. The ruling planet of Pisces, our most mystical, visionary, and otherworldly sign, it makes sense that Jupiter is Pisces' ruler, as Jupiter functions to expand us beyond limits, including those of the material world. As the animating spirit of Pisces, Jupiter is associated with gaining spiritual knowledge and wisdom, as well as personal growth and abundance.

Jupiter Shadow Qualities

Just as heroes can be flawed and villains full of unexpected sympathies, Jupiter ultimately represents a complex energy. The darker side of Jupiter influences us to be wasteful and indulgent. In this respect, keep in mind that Jupiter also rules over Sagittarius, a fire sign known for its adventurism. Behind this cavalier Sagittarius attitude, we find Jupiterian energy in a different guise: heedless and somewhat reckless.

Life on the Jupiter Line

Full. Optimistic. Easy. Things going your way. You've had those moments in life, or those exceedingly good days, where you feel a bit more buoyant and supported by some kind of cosmic zephyr. That feeling of ease characterises Jupiter line energy.

The Jupiter line is like getting dealt a great hand in poker. While everyone can benefit from the good tidings that Jupiter brings, this is a line that might be especially beneficial if you're feeling down on your luck or pessimistic, or if you're concerned about life's options seeming too narrow. Jupiter energy can help provide the ultimate glass-half full perspective on yourself and others.

By consciously connecting with Jupiter's energy, you can enhance these positive attributes, attracting more luck and favourable circumstances into your life. Whether through travel, personal development, or simply adopting a more optimistic mindset, your Jupiter line can help you turn your fortunes around and seize the opportunities that come your way.

To fully engage with this energy, consider immersing yourself in these places, whether physically or through other forms of exploration like literature, cultural experiences, or virtual engagements. It's about syncing with the expansive spirit of these locations, allowing their energy to enhance your own.

**TRAVELLING ON
YOUR JUPITER LINE**

BEST FOR
luck; celebrating major milestones; expanding your social circle; indulging in soul-seeking experiences; growth; abundance; attracting good fortune; pursuing positive thinking; and enlarging your horizons in every way, whether it's through travel, learning, or personal development.

WHAT TO PLAN
look for social opportunities; sample culinary delights; visit cultural landmarks, grand architecture or a sprawling park; or attend a lively festival.

WHAT TO PACK
regal, royal purple clothing; an uplifting, expansive fragrance like frankincense to channel Jupiter's holy, abundant energy; and Tolstoy's *War and Peace*, an expansive book that will fill your mind with a sense of life's epic scale.

The Jupiter
AC ——————— Personal Line

Risk. Sometimes it's a good thing. I had a client who felt the straits
of his life were narrowing; there was too much pressure at work and
not enough time for his true passion, jazz piano. We talked about
exploring his Jupiter personal line and how he could take a break
from responsibility to enlarge his sense of possibility.

In an act of boldness, which, of course, fortune favours, he moved
to a spot on his Jupiter line with little hesitation. Risky, indeed. But
a powerful choice. Upon settling to one of his Jupiterian hot spots, he
found a new job that was much less restrictive. Instead of managing a
team of ten, he was flourishing in a contributor role. The money was
less, but he was rich in time and able to pursue his passion without
the discord of workplace obligations in his life.

The Jupiter personal line is for those who may likewise be feeling
hemmed in. It's for those who colour inside the lines, yet need a new,
larger canvas for self-expression.

ELEVATE YOUR PASSIONS

It's time to get off social media and open up your world to art, literature, and film. There's a nobility to Jupiter's influence. It tends toward upscaled forms of knowledge. Life on the Jupiter personal line suggests a time to expose yourself to cultural experiences beyond your usual purview.

BET ON YOURSELF

In the world of sports, athletes will often bet on themselves during a contract year (meaning they may take less money now, thinking that after a good season, they will triple their money in negotiations down the road). Do the same on your Jupiter personal line – it will pay off.

BECOME SANTA

Sure, life on your Jupiter line should attract largesse your way, but what about you, friend? Don't be that grumpy coworker sitting at your cubicle. Be that Jupiterian figure who shows up to work with some Persian desserts you made in your cooking class last night and pass those confections around.

AVOID BURNOUT

Life on the Jupiter personal line can have us brimming with confidence, but don't get too caught up in your new world of social charm and end up burnt out, over-saturated and over-extended. Why? Because you can't be as charming and attract Jupiterian opportunity when you're tired.

The Jupiter
DC ———— Relationship Line

I have a client who had terrible luck with romantic relationships. During an astrocartography session, we talked about her exploring her Jupiter relationship line to help bring joy and opportunity to her love life. Needing a fresh start, she moved to one of her Jupiter power places for relationships. Within a couple months she fell in love with someone deeply and lastingly. She also began a business partnership with someone else that involved founding an artist management agency, illustrating how the Jupiter relationship line isn't just for romantic pairings, but also significant, long-term business partnerships.

For those who are looking for abundance that comes from one-on-one magic, or who are struggling with their romantic options, this line could help activate the largesse that comes from the Jupiterian concept of "more".

ENGAGE IN VOLUNTEER WORK

Volunteering for causes you care about not only enriches your life but introduces you to compassionate, community-minded individuals who are Jupiterian in spirit and action.

SAY "YES"

Jupiter never inspires us to say "no" – it's a blessing and a curse. But being on a Jupiter line is about saying "yes" as much as possible, even if that yes is outside your comfort zone. Attend block parties, dinner parties, social gatherings, and events where you can expand your social circle. Expansion = Jupiter.

STAY POSITIVE AND OPEN-MINDED

Jupiter's influence is optimistic and expansive. Embrace the possibilities and trust that the right person will come into your life at the right time. Sometimes things can take a while. Instant gratification is sort of boring anyway.

KEEP IT IN THE POCKET

Remember that Jupiter can be excessive. Don't overindulge with a romantic partner and lose yourself by giving too much of yourself. Maintain "me time" at all costs.

The Jupiter

MC —————— Career Line

Kim Kardashian has her Jupiter career line running through where she resides (LA), which gives us a sense of how the Planet of Abundance impacts power places related to professional life. In the context of career, this might manifest in feeling like work is easy, or cash coming without much effort. Or sometimes, it's about being in the right place with the right connections. Kim's first big break came from organizing Paris Hilton's closet. Access is everything.

Jupiter's influence also signifies expansion, potentially leading to fortunate opportunities like catching a big break. You might find yourself in the right place at the right time, gaining unexpected access to auditions or opportunities.

The Jupiter career line is for people who are ready to step sinto a bigger role with their vocation, and those who are struggling with fears or anxieties around their career path. It can push us to go beyond limiting self-concepts, and provide optimism where we might otherwise feel unease.

CHASE GIGS THAT PUSH YOU

On your Jupiter career line, it's all about finding roles that stretch you beyond your skillset. Look for positions that make you sweat a little. This is not a line for simple stuff you've already mastered.

SCHOOL YOURSELF, BUT MAKE IT FUN
To get beyond your skillset, the Jupiter career line supports life of the mind (in addition to the grind), so dive into courses or certifications that excite you. Feed your brain.

NETWORK, NETWORK, NETWORK
The Jupiter career line can attract attention to you, but it also supports you being more proactive. This might be hard if you are someone who tends to be more passive. Get beyond that and take a step forward.

CAREERS SUPPORTED BY JUPITER

TRAVEL & TOURISM	Travel writers, cultural ambassadors, and event planners who explore and share the wonders of the world.
LAW & JUSTICE	Policy reformers, human rights advocates, and judicial leaders who work towards justice are auspicious on this line.
PUBLISHING & MEDIA	Authors, editors, and media strategists who influence public discourse and ideas, and expand ideas through media.
ACADEMIA & RESEARCH	Roles that expand the mind through the understanding of complex ideas that come with study are supported here.
PHILANTHROPY	NGO leaders, social entrepreneurs, and community organizers who drive meaningful social change.

The Jupiter Home Line

IC

A few years ago, I relocated to Berlin because my Jupiter home line runs through this wonderful city. When I got here, I felt like the world opened up for me. It's hard to get a place in Berlin, but I was fortunate enough to live in an apartment rent-free for two years through work, and chanced upon my forever home randomly from a friend.

Luck for someone on the Jupiter home line can manifest in various ways, from amazing opportunities in buying or selling property, to expanding your family size or linking up with good contractors or interior designers, who will help realize your vision. This line is for those who might be looking around your place right now and thinking: maybe it's time for an upgrade.

SPOT REAL ESTATE OPPORTUNITIES

Luck in real estate can come from immersing yourself in your Jupiterian power places with all their bustle and angles. Those with their Jupiter line activated could attract opportunities that others are missing.

DECLUTTER

Life on the Jupiter home line can help you find epic spaces, but maybe the best space for you is a snug, Tokyo-inspired one with amazing built-in closets for efficiency. Declutter to make even your small space feel large and Jupiterian.

MAXIMAL, NOT MINIMAL

Expect interior and exterior spaces on this line to feel sumptuous, richly decorated, and perhaps even overly appointed with possessions. Minimal, neutral, and clinical design will be ceded to maximal or ornate details bespeaking the planet's abundant nature.

FORGE COMMUNITY BONDS

Immerse yourself in a community where real connections thrive. Seek out neighbourhoods where support and camaraderie are genuine. Get involved in local events, join groups that align with your passions.

The Jupiter home line is for those thinking: maybe it's time for a change and an upgrade.

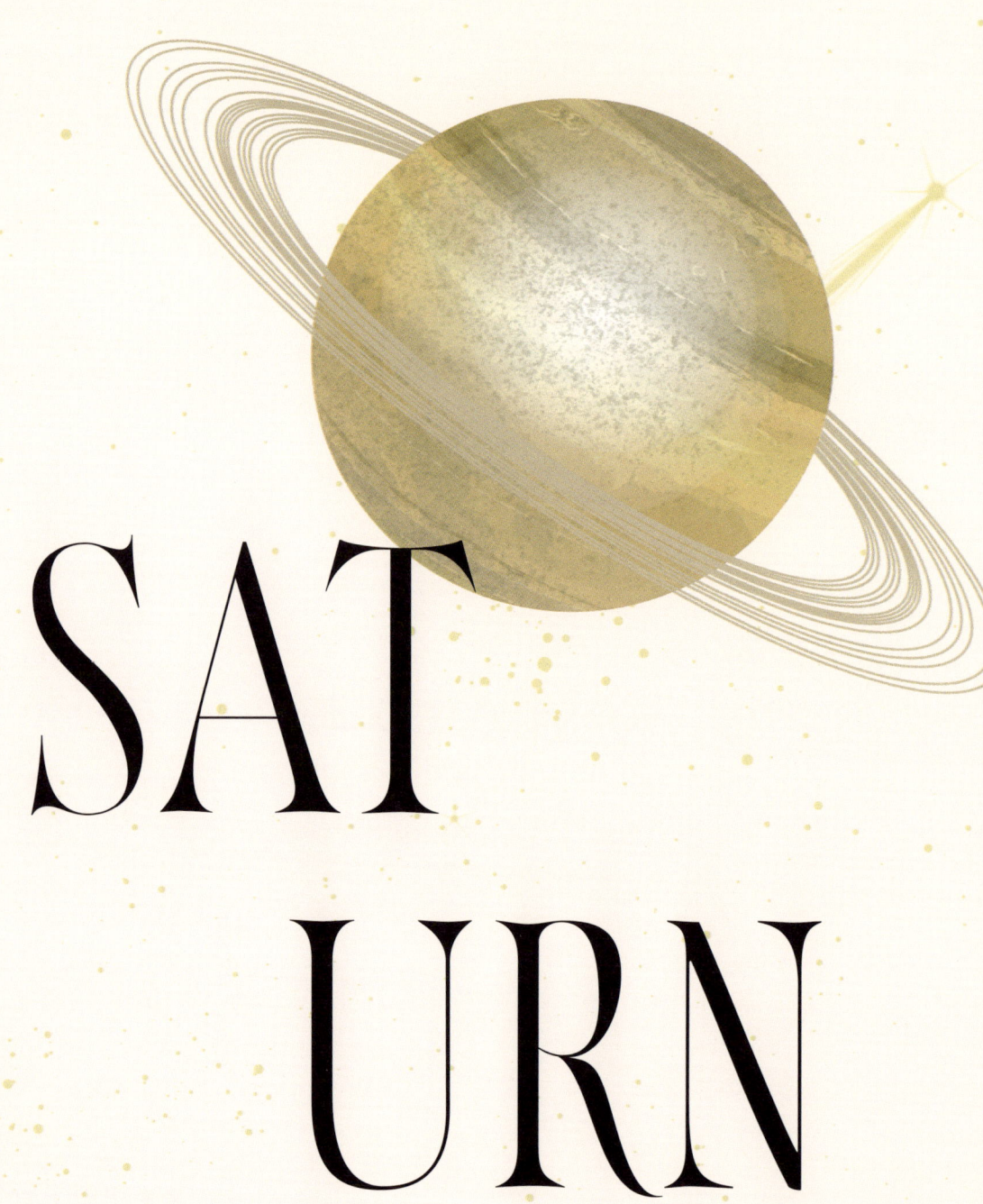

SAT
URN

Discipline | Structure | Responsibility
Tradition | Boundaries | Order

The Saturn line signifies power places where you may feel more orderly, patient, and structured in your approach to long-term projects or goals. Those who live on or visit their Saturn lines may experience increased determination to meet and overcome challenges. While the Saturn line may feel demanding, it encourages personal development through hard work, discipline, and perseverance, ultimately mapping locations that require you to be mature and get serious about career, home, work, and love.

The Planet of Less

Saturn is also known as the taskmaster, disciplinarian, schoolmaster, and "Great Malefic". Though this tough planet is often seen as a pessimistic and melancholic influence, this doesn't mean its presence in your life will lead to doom. Depending on your birth chart, Saturn can bring stability, where in someone else's, it might portend tougher luck. Life also isn't always about avoiding challenges, but meeting them, and this planet requires effort, labour, commitment, and responsibility. Essentially, Saturn's line are for grown-ups.

Saturn's Light Qualities

In its more positive valences, Saturn can provide structure, containment, law, limits, and order, and give life a sense of regularity and rhythm. It's also about grind, work ethic, and discipline, and stands for longevity and distant returns on investment. You have to earn your keep with Saturn, as there are no handouts here, but there is something old school and hearty about this side to Saturn. It is ultimately fair.

Saturn's Shadow Qualities

Saturn's negative qualities can be boiled down to one word: loss. Where Jupiter is the planet of gain and excess, Saturn's role in the cosmic order is to take away or to subtract. Saturn's influence can therefore shade into pessimistic attitudes and behaviours like depression, melancholia, or world-weariness. The ancients said that those born under Saturn grow up to have crooked shoulders, as if from bearing some existential weight over decades.

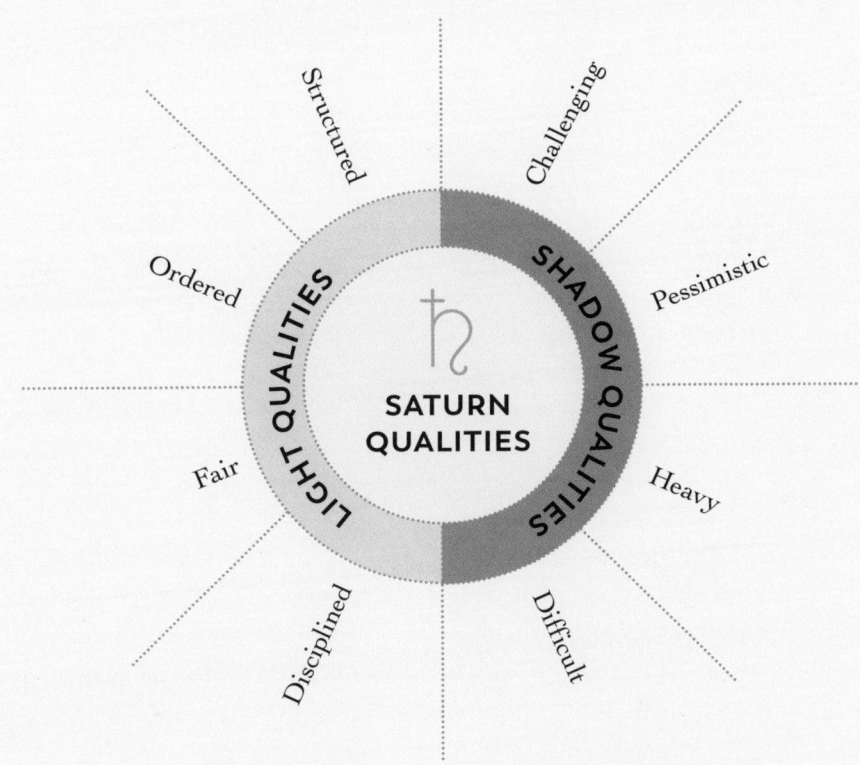

Life on the Saturn Line

Heavy. Challenging. Ordered. I like to tell my clients that being on a Saturn line is like lifting weights to get stronger: it's not easy, but it's deeply rewarding with time. In a culture of instant gratification, this message of Saturnal delay may not seem to be the easiest sell. But surprisingly, I've found many people seek the weightiness of the Saturn line.

In modern life, we can be confronted by the paradox of freedom, whereby we are required not only to submit ourselves to duty, but to figure out what our duty is to begin with. That's hard. The Saturn line – with its emphasis on order and structure – can help allay the anxieties associated with this form of modern freedom, and its power places are for those who crave responsibility and stability amid the chaotic flux of contemporary life.

This line can help you stay focused, work hard, and achieve long-term success. When relocating to or visiting your Saturn line, you may experience an intensified sense of obligation towards yourself and others. Ultimately, this line is for those who may be feeling weak, lost, or unmoored, but who gradually want to get stronger, more resilient, and more grounded.

TRAVELLING ON YOUR SATURN LINE

BEST FOR
solitude and introspection; breaking from the chaos; making significant decisions; wanting to focus on long-term goals without distractions; planning; getting serious about your ambitions; or learning from the past.

WHAT TO PLAN
visits to historical monuments; completing a PhD; or solo trips focused on setting and planning your intentions for the coming year.

WHAT TO PACK
black clothes; earthy perfumes or essential oils like vetiver and spikenard; and Hannah Arendt's *The Origins of Totalitarianism*, which is austere, rigorous, serious, and rewarding.

The Saturn
AC ——————— Personal Line

Back to basics. This is the line you go to when you realize that your life has gotten too busy, ornamented, frilly, or playful. Here, you wake up, read, meditate, and keep your possessions to a minimum. You stick to a strict schedule, eat simple dishes, and sleep on a bed with a single pillow.

Your responsibility is to yourself on this line. No excuses, no distractions. Solitude becomes a sanctuary, and in the stillness of your life, you can see your missteps clearly, and better navigate a direction toward firmer ground. What's more, you will find the inner strength now to make that trek, where before you may have been scattered, undisciplined, and sleeping past 9a.m. on a bed with eight pillows (which, on this line, is seven pillows too many).

GROW UP
This is a serious line, so expect to start looking at your life in terms of long-term arcs rather than quick gains. Part of the maturity process here will be a more practical approach to your world, as youthful ideals may yield to more mature concerns like mortgages and public school systems for your eventual children.

MAINTAIN HIGH STANDARDS
Expect to hold yourself to higher standards here than on other lines, and to be more critical for not meeting these standards. Just be careful not to be too hard on yourself.

MANAGE YOUR TIME
If your life lacks direction, use this line to provide discipline in the form of rule-based routines or strict schedules that give shape and structure to your days.

BE PRUDENT
Be cautious in your decisions and actions. If you're having trouble with impulse-control or excessive pleasure-seeking, Saturnal power places may help slow down this tendency, fostering the fortitude that comes with prudence.

The Saturn
DC ——— Relationship Line

Like wine, relationships on your Saturn relationship line will age nicely, and this means that you should consider the Saturn relationship line if you're looking for long-term commitments that ripen over the years.

Saturn's association with time and longevity also may have you attracted to older people on this line. The relationship dynamics on the Saturn line could, therefore, revolve around you learning valuable life lessons from an older partner. Romantic relationships may feel more like mentorship programs at times. Or, in the realm of business relationships, you may find incredible mentors who help you grow your professional knowledge along Saturnal power places. If you're sensing a somewhat anti-romantic quality to this line, your perceptions would be correct.

GO STEADY
Head to this line if you're looking to find a serious relationship rather than a casual, ambiguous, or non-committed affair. This doesn't mean that relationships will be boring, but rather that you can rely on your partner to share and develop a life together.

OWN UP

On this line, expect not only to meet people who are responsible, but people who take responsibility for their actions, too. There is a difference here; a partner who financially provides for a family (responsible) may never take responsibility for dysfunction they have contributed to a partnership. So if you're looking for someone who owns up to their actions, consider this line.

EMBRACE TRADITION

Expect to feel a bit more old-fashioned when it comes to relationships here. This doesn't mean you need to adopt ideals you don't believe in, but rather, you may find yourself developing a preference for conventional forms of commitment like marriage, home-owning, or shared bank accounts.

The Saturn

Career Line

Queen Elizabeth II's Saturn career line ran through London, where she served as queen for the longest reign in British history. Duration signals one of Saturn's chief qualities, so the length of Elizabeth's reign feels particularly fitting here. The queen's leadership style was likewise Saturnal: unwavering, founded on respect for tradition, and with no frills, despite the majestic opulence associated with the crown.

While you may not be at your job for 70 years like Elizabeth was, you should move to your Saturn career line if you're looking for longevity and stability with your career. Ultimately, this is a line for those looking to be quietly ambitious, discrete, and dutiful at work, where respect through honest endeavour and reliability will take precedence over gaining a reputation for the dazzling.

BE A COMPANY PLAYER

On this line, expect to value the sense of order, authority, and hierarchy that comes with typically successful workplace environments or institutions. You will likely be more drawn to jobs that offer these kinds of stable structures rather than careers governed by a risk-taking mentality.

BUILD INCREMENTAL SUCCESS

Allow your rise to be slow and steady on this line, and prepare for success to come later in life. This isn't a line where you tend to receive instant recognition, so a long-haul mentality is favoured here.

EXPECT CHALLENGES

Saturn brings challenges and setbacks, so you may find that despite a reputation for hard work and responsibility, you still encounter career obstacles on this line. Go here to build character and resilience rather than a weak, untested, and cloistered virtue.

CAREERS SUPPORTED BY SATURN

ARCHITECTURE & ENGINEERING	Professions that build things from the ground up or efficiently organize things will be particularly supported here.
AGRICULTURE	Saturn has long been associated with the earth, symbolizing farming, gardening, and cultivating.
FINANCE & ACCOUNTING	Professions related to the meticulous nature around finances and long-term planning will tend to be auspicious here.
MANAGEMENT	Management consultants, strategic planners, and operations managers that focus on improving organizational structure may flourish on this line.

The Saturn

IC ——————— Home Line

I was born on my Saturn home line, and I lived a wonderful though rather Saturnal childhood in the countryside of Ireland. Kids my age were scarce, so I spent a lot of time alone, except for being with my family. This sense of relative isolation provides a bit of insight into the Saturn home line, where you tend to find nothing extraneous.

This isn't to say that life on your Saturn home line has to be lonely. Instead, you may find that you are almost forced to focus on the things that matter. Growing up, I was all about school, studying, reading, and writing, and now that I'm older, I particularly cherish the Saturnal nature of my homecoming in that home remains a place for writing, discipline, and work.

For some, life on their Saturn home line may tend more towards an intensified sense of duty towards family, where you play the role of manager. The deep, emotional warmth of, say, the Moon home line may be less expressed here, as you act in a more reserved way of parenting to inculcate discipline or moral codes.

BUILD STRONG FOUNDATIONS

Think of Saturn as a builder; it's all about providing solid foundations. On this line, this energy can manifest in you literally constructing a home from the ground up, or starting a family with you as a strong, morally upright source of lessons and guidance.

FOCUS ON LEGACY-BUILDING

On this line, leaving a legacy becomes more important. Saturn's long-term vision will tend to have you looking ahead, so develop family traditions, engage in estate planning, and build sustainable environmental practices that will help the community at large.

CHOOSE QUALITY OVER QUANTITY

As opposed to the decorative excesses on the Jupiter line, here, keep your living environment decluttered, essential, and tastefully restrained. In general, home life will tend to be quiet, stable, and elegant, with a hint of formality.

Life on the Saturn home line may tend towards an intensified sense of duty towards family, where you play the role of manager.

URA
NUS

Innovation | Independence
Vision | Forward-Thinking

The Uranus line charts power places where you may experience sudden changes that break with your established routines or expectations. Those who visit or live on their Uranus lines may also feel more open to or interested in exploring alternative lifestyles. Encouraging you to get out of your comfort zone, locations along the Uranus line foster creative thinking and problem-solving. While the Uranus line may be destabilizing and strange at times, it is precisely this unorthodox energy that allows for personal growth.

The Planet of Strange Happenings

Generally, the following planets dominate astrological discourse: communicative Mercury, lovely Venus, caffeinated Mars, generous Jupiter, strict Saturn, the vital Sun, and the emotional Moon. But for those looking for a different kind of line, Uranus energy represents the road less taken. Uranus keeps things off balance, offering up surprises and generating wildcard energy. Even its planetary rotation is odd. Astronomically, it basically spins on its side. And symbolically, it marches to the beat of its own drum, tapping out rhythms in an odd 7/4 time beat.

Uranus's Light Qualities

Uranus is associated with radical change and revolution, and can express itself through innovation, futuristic-thinking or leftfield ideas. In a political sense, it tends to manifest through political activism and progressive causes in the service of non-conformity and equality. Uranus is also about breaking free from social constraints, hence its reputation for having a quirky influence.

Uranus's Shadow Qualities

The random and unorthodox nature of Uranus may manifest in its darker valences as unpredictability and instability. As a planetary energy that tends towards cerebral thinking, it also represents emotional detachment or eccentric behaviour that makes you somewhat unapproachable or unrelatable. Uranus can also cause sudden, disruptive events that throw life off-balance, which may be jarring, and can cause professional upheaval or relationship breakdowns.

Life on the Uranus Line

Unpredictable. Innovative. Quirky. Life on the Uranus line might look surprising. Here, doing something outside of your usual routine will be cosmically supported, leading to unexpected but auspicious events. Ultimately, the Uranus line is for those open to the exciting and unpredictable side of life.

While your world here may feel slightly off-kilter like the axis of Uranus itself, if you're willing to embrace it, your world may shift in powerful new ways. The key to working with Uranus's energy is to embrace its gifts of ingenuity, originality, and out-of-the-box thinking, while also remaining grounded with clear career or relationship goals.

Uranus invites you to break free from constraints, but it's important to ensure that these changes serve a positive, meaningful purpose. This makes it the line to visit or relocate to if you're looking to enliven a spirit of anti-establishment activism, or engage in work that seeks to redress inequalities to create a more just and equal cosmic order.

BEST FOR
breaking out of a rut; letting loose; being free; walking on the wild side; exploring alternative lifestyles and identities; rebelling from bourgeois norms and structures; spontaneous encounters; doing things differently; or moving beyond comfort zones.

TRAVELLING ON YOUR URANUS LINE

WHAT TO PLAN
attend tech conferences; explore cutting-edge art; dive into futuristic projects; embrace spontaneity; challenge conventions; or mix up your plans by embracing a less rigid itinerary in favour of exciting, uncharted adventures.

WHAT TO PACK
clothes for all four seasons, since you never know what you're going to get with Uranus; your quirkiest teal attire; and *The Pillow Book* by Sei Shōnagon, a marvel of observations and poetry written by a lady-in-waiting amid the courtly life in Heian-era Japan.

The Uranus
AC —————— Personal Line

Power places on your Uranus personal line will tend to stir in you a political consciousness, and with it a will for radical change to oppressive power structures. Scholar and political activist Angela Davis has her Uranus personal line running through New York City, where, as part of a Southern Black student exchange program, her fight for racial and gender equality took incipient form. This is undoubtedly a line for those who are looking to change the world in some way for the better.

If you are also interested in exploring new forms of self-expression like gender nonconformity, or looking to develop your avant-garde aesthetics and tastes, this line may be for you.

SEEK MORE FREEDOM

Expect to be more freedom-conscious here, and to nurture an awakened independence that respects and fights for difference in all its glorious forms.

EMBRACE UNPREDICTABILITY

On this line, allow yourself to be more spontaneous in thought and action. You may also develop unconventional ideas about culture, politics, and society.

DISCOVER THE WEIRD

Be open-minded to weirder forms of art, novels,
music, and film as you broaden your sense of what
is possible through sounds, words, and images.

LOOK TO THE FUTURE

While other planetary lines may find great succour
in the past, expect to be resolutely forward-thinking,
when it comes to your interests. You will tend to think
about and live for a better future rather than the past.

The Uranus
DC ──────── Relationship Line

On this line, unconventionality reigns. Relationships here may be structured in untraditional ways, and you may be attracted to quirkier partners who will open your world to a new world of cultural referents and experiences.

As such, partners on this line will tend to expand your knowledge base. You may both travel, and relationships could also be more open or experimental, as you explore love triangles and other such configurations of desire and affection.

Friendships on this line can likewise lean towards unique types, and living arrangements that might develop from these friendships can equally be out-of-the-ordinary for you, such as co-op living or other forward-thinking modes of togetherness. Ultimately, this is a line for those looking for eccentricity in friends and lovers.

FALL IN (STRANGE) LOVE

Every relationship has its own weird routines, secret languages, and unique forms of intimacy. But this line will turn the strange up to 11. Expect to attract off-kilter partners who help you look at the world from their odd angles, while you become the better for it.

MAKE SPACE

Expect to attract relationships on this line that require room to grow. Learning to love at a distance characterizes a key feature of this line, and learning to respect both your and your partner's need for space is key here.

BRACE FOR SUDDEN CHANGES

Uranus can cause abrupt shifts in our life. In the context of relationships, prepare for sudden circumstances that push your relationship to deeper levels of intimacy than you had planned.

CHOOSE YOUR HEAD OVER YOUR HEART

On this line, expect thrilling discussions about big topics as you intellectualize the days and nights away. A more analytical approach to emotions and the avoidance of mawkish displays of sentimentality can work well on this line, too.

The Uranus
—————— Career Line

There are a few paths that life on the Uranus career line might take you down. If you are a free spirit, you may like to relocate to one of your power places with no preconceptions or plans, and simply trust that something unique or unexpected awaits you career-wise.

You can also seek out power places on your Uranus career line for a relocation or visit to achieve some kind of breakthrough or innovation in a project, as a major shift in perspective may occur in your research on this line.

Or, you may wish to use the Uranus career line to make progressive social change, as careers that work to upend oppressive norms will be supported here. The through-line in each of these approaches is empowerment through non-conformity.

SEEK UNORTHODOX WORKSTATIONS
Avoid typical office settings on this line. This might mean boycotting environments where hierarchy is levelled and egalitarianism functions as guiding ethos. Here, work should feel dynamic with the potential for sudden changes.

WORK REMOTELY
The plight of people half a world away might occupy your time, or work that analyses the future (rather than the present) may become a focus here. Expect to think global and act global as the local becomes less of a concern on this line.

BE TECH SAVVY

Ask more questions concerning technology on this line. Careers that track, develop, inveigh against, or monitor tech will be supported here, or you may use technology to enable skill-building, optimize resource use, or provide better support to organizations interfacing with marginalized communities.

REBEL

Authority will tend to irk you on this line, so expect to fight not only for your vision and causes, but for your right to do work your way, at your own pace, with your own methods.

CAREERS SUPPORTED BY URANUS

TRENDSETTING	Careers that identify and ignite cultural, technological, and social trends as they relate to humanity are auspicious on this line.
URBAN GREEN DESIGN	A career that helps redefine how cities harmonize with nature (rather than subordinate it) embodies Uranus energy.
ENVIRONMENTAL, SOCIAL, & HUMAN RIGHTS	Working on issues pertaining to LGBTQ+ rights, environmental justice, or prison reform aligns with Uranus energy.
ALTERNATIVE HEALING	Careers in holistic healthcare that embrace unorthodox methods in wellness will be particularly supported here.

The Uranus

IC ———— Home Line

The Uranus home line represents your emotional foundation, your family life, and your sense of security. When impacted by the wildcard energy of Uranus, this line can be characterized by unpredictability, innovation, and the breaking of traditional family structures as you seek to revolutionize old routines and lend your private life new shape.

Here, the way you structure your family dynamics or your personal living space may be unique. Living in power places on your Uranus home line may also involve frequent change and movement, as this planet is one of sudden shifts. This might mean relocations and renovations as they relate to your lived environment.

The rebellious side of Uranus could also manifest in a home that is especially engaged politically, while adolescent children may be particularly at loggerheads with parental authority.

EXPERIMENT AESTHETICALLY

Favour spaces with an unorthodox layout, eschewing traditional décor aesthetics in favour of unexpected materials like repurposed eco-modern features and structures, odd furniture, and art objects that speak to an avant-futurism.

BE UNTRADITIONAL

Prioritize your own ideas of independence and unconventional living on this line, thereby challenging the notion of a stable, traditional home life. Curfew, bedtimes, and breakfast are all symptoms of bourgeois thought, and in need of revision.

EXPLORE GADGETRY

On this line of innovation, expect your home to be hooked up to technologies and gadgets that make life seem more futuristic. Such an interest may develop from you, your partner, or your children, leading your home towards the 23rd century.

EMBRACE THE RANDOM

Unlike the calm you might find on the Saturn home line, expect the energy here to be more randomized. This could mean that your home feels like a hub for unexpected guests, last-minute parties, or ad hoc intellectual get-togethers to discuss political strategies.

The Uranus home line can be characterized by unpredictability, innovation and the breaking of traditional family structures.

NEP TUNE

Imagination | Intuition | Mystery
Growth Through Fantasy

The Neptune line points to power places where you may experience intensified desires for spiritual-seeking and transcendence. Those who live on or visit their Neptune line may feel more idealistic and utopian, finding themselves drawn to metaphysical questions and practices. Artistic tendencies may be enlivened in Neptunian power places as well. While it may lead to a sense of escapism or withdrawal from the world, the Neptune line ultimately suggests locations that invite exploration of spiritual realities beyond it.

The Planet of Fantasy

"Dreaming big" captures the essence of Neptune, a planet whose impact on our lives has to do with transcendence, idealism, and searching for utopias, whether in love, work, or community. It's influence also leads us towards greater dimensions, be it through art, fantasy, spiritual enlightenment, or delusions of grandeur. With Neptune in the picture, the practicality of the "here and now" vanishes in the great beyond. Named after the God of the Sea in Roman mythology, Neptune is associated with oceanic experiences that take us beyond the tidy shorelines of our understanding.

Neptune's Light Qualities

Neptune inspires creativity, compassion, and spiritual awareness. It helps us connect to our imagination, enhances creativity, and facilitates self-expression through creative work. People with strong Neptune placements in their birth chart may feel naturally drawn to mystical concepts, often having a vivid inner dreamlife and a desire to escape ordinary reality through creative expression.

Neptune's Shadow Qualities

The Neptunian impulse to go beyond the here and now for something more otherworldly could portend to addictive behaviour that aims, in its own way, to transcend the hardships of existence through escapism. The shadow side to Neptune, may then lead into indifference toward responsibility. A transfixation on glamour to the point of self-delusion is another shadow-side to Neptune's influence.

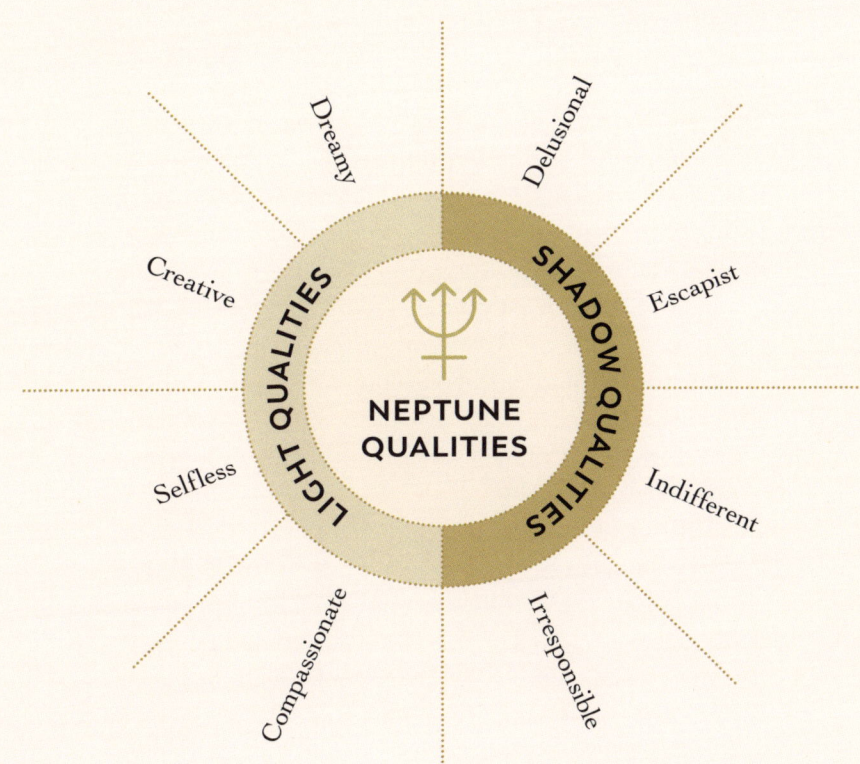

Life on the Neptune Line

Dreamy. Insightful. Otherworldly. Letting go is the mantra of life on the Neptune line, and unlike the loss we can encounter on the Saturn line (where we may be forced to let go of things through hardship), letting go on the Neptune line means letting go of things we want to get rid of in exchange for peace, insight, and awakening.

I like to think of life on the Neptune line as a kind of spiritual yard sale, where we sell stuff for cheap, but are left with the glory of an uncluttered soul. In my consultations, I've found that those really searching for spiritual insight tend to want to know more about where their Neptune line laces around the globe, like the subtle skeins of incense in sacred spaces.

Whether it's in romance, work, home life, or personal development, people who reside on or visit their Neptune line typically find that their lives are infused with a greater connection to the mystical aspects of life. The influence of the Neptune line, therefore, makes this line perfect for individuals looking to live a life that feels surreal and dreamlike, and looks beyond the material world.

TRAVELLING ON YOUR NEPTUNE LINE

BEST FOR

getting spiritual; shamanistic journeys; dissolving the ego; becoming one; creativity; transcendence; renouncing the world; metaphysical explorations; healing and peace; recharging; or diving deep into cosmic consciousness.

WHAT TO PLAN

meditation practices; yoga classes; dancing; visits to sacred art structures; or healing rituals.

WHAT TO PACK

flowy clothes; a lilac dream journal; *Autobiography of a Yogi* by Paramahansa Yogananda; tarot cards; and body paint, glitter, or anything that glows at night.

The Neptune
Personal Line

There is a delicious paradox on this line: in order to develop yourself, you must in some profound way lose yourself. The Neptune personal line is about letting go of possessions, anger, jealousies, and whatever keeps you attached to a world you seek to go beyond. If this sounds appealing, this line may be for you.

On this line, connect to places where spiritual guidance is readily available, such as meditation centres, ashrams, and qualified teachers, rather than opting for solo vision quests. To thrive here, find supportive practices that help you balance your idealism and spiritual questing with practical self-care and grounding. Uplifting and safe practices here only.

EMBRACE NON-LINEAR THINKING

On this line, expect enhanced intuitive perception, making you more skilled in understanding deeper unconscious needs. Your connection to the unconscious mind may also allow access to non-linear or symbolic understandings of the world, which can be a valuable asset in creative problem-solving.

BE FLEXIBLE

Learn to become more comfortable with ups and downs here, while remaining less tied to rigid structures or expectations. Neptune is the ultimate flowy energy, and by aligning with it, you can move beyond the joys and pains that come with attachment to loss and impermanence.

DON'T LOSE YOUR SELF

Neptune's potential to dissolve rigid self-definitions may make you susceptible to a chameleonlike quality here. This is something to be aware of, as it may lead to a sense of confusion about your own identity.

GO WITH THE FLOW

You may like to adopt a personal aesthetic that is somewhat loose, bohemian, or free-flowing here, like scarves, billowing linen, and other deconstructed styles whose designs feel inspired by nature. This style may serve to reflect self-presentation as a mystical or ethereal.

The Neptune
Relationship Line

DC ———

Neptune blurs boundaries. Accordingly, this can be a tricky relationship line, as here, you may become less willing to give a partner space, desiring instead to merge into some kind of mystical union of souls. You may also be more attracted to people who are bad with boundaries.

Idealizing a love interest or refusing to see them for who they really are might pose problems on this line. Ignoring warning signs in favour of co-dependency or the ecstasy of romance, you may also run the risk of becoming an easy target for suspicious characters.

These strong caveats aside, however, this line can be a powerful place to find your deepest, most intuitive and soulful connections. In addition, this line may also prove especially rich if you're looking for spiritual sojourners who, like you, are interested in accessing transcendental realities.

EXPECT HAZY BOUNDARIES

Relationships may feel ethereal on this line, and romantic expectations as they pertain to fidelity may be hazy and unclear. You or your partner may be more inclined to act out fantasies beyond the confines of traditional coupledom, and while such indeterminacy may be a thrill, it may also need to be clearly addressed. Sometimes unspoken understandings need to be spoken about.

BE COMPASSIONATE

Expect your sense of compassion to be heightened on this line, as you are more prone to provide love, time, and understanding for friends and romantic partners. However, be mindful of relationships where you give more than you receive.

SING IN HARMONY

In addition to spiritual searchers, expect to be drawn to musical or artistic types who create vast worlds of sound or image. If you're likewise musically minded, relationships here could flourish through chordal harmonies, as well as those of the heart.

The Neptune Career Line

This is not a line you go to if you're interested in work that relies on traditional metrics such as project completion rate, revenue generation, and other key performance indicators. Instead, think of this line as somewhat of a New Age energy, where compassion and humanitarianism are of more value than profit margins. This isn't to say that money can't be made here, but this should not be a motivating factor.

Ultimately, the Neptune career line invites you to engage in work that tries to create new worlds that bring collective fulfilment through the power of art, love, or peace-seeking. If this dreamy utopianism for a potential career captures your imagination, this line could be a powerful place to manifest a vocation aligned with your values, creativity, and empathetic investment in the greater good.

PURSUE DREAM JOBS

On this line, careers related to dreams, dreaming, and the dreamworld will be supported. Pursue jobs that encourage your creativity and imagination to blossom into reality like art, music, or creative writing.

BE A VISIONARY

Expect your reputation at work to be something of a visionary, as the energy on this line tends to make you seem mysterious, with access to heightened forms of intuition or understanding.

THINK ASHRAM, NOT OFFICE

Given the spiritual influence of Neptune, expect careers here to flourish in worksites outside of traditional environments. Vocations that centre around ashrams, churches, meccas, pilgrimages, and other such sacred spaces or journeys will all be strengthened on this line.

OFFER SELFLESS SERVICE

Look for ways to support humanitarian, spiritual, or religious causes within your career in some way on this line. While careers in these specific fields tend not to pay well, you'll receive bonus points for heaven or good karma by working in them.

CAREERS SUPPORTED BY NEPTUNE

THE ARTS
Consider this line to find cosmic support as an artist, creative writer, illustrator, or performer.

HUMANITARIANISM
Careers in humanitarian fields such as social work or global aid initiatives are well supported on this line.

CREATIVE MANAGEMENT
Working with artists, musicians, or writers will channel Neptune's empathy, helping creative talents navigate their careers.

WELLNESS
Careers such as meditation teacher, yoga instructor, or spiritual guide are well attuned to this line.

The Neptune

IC ——— Home Line

Neptune's energy tends to make a rooted home life somewhat difficult, as a permanent residence or stable family structures could be harder to establish here. You may feel like you're never really at home in a traditional sense. That's to be expected when you're on a planetary line that pulls you toward oceanic, spiritual experiences.

Since Neptune encourages compassion and empathy, family dynamics will tend to be supportive and caring here – though you may need to create boundaries to avoid becoming overwhelmed by the energies of others emotional demands. Despite your efforts at boundary-making, being on time to school may be a problem here, as routines may be hard to institute. Rather than fighting this tendency towards tardiness, this line will encourage you to embrace a home life that operates on its own time, off the grid and clock.

BE SENSITIVE TO YOUR SURROUNDINGS

This line could make you highly sensitive to the energy at home, so expect to become more attuned, for better or worse, to shifts in mood or ambiance. This can help cultivate an empathetic environment.

LOOK TO THE SEA

Expect an intensified desire to be near bodies of water on this line. This will activate Neptunian energy, encourage introspection, and issue forth creativity and calm. This line is all about matching the oceanic ebb and flow of shorelines and soul lines.

EMBRACE MOOD LIGHTING

Explore open concept living spaces, low lighting, soft chanting on your sound system, and gentle decorative elements that invoke a sense of peace on this line. Hard edges, moody or dark colour palettes, and clinical or overly minimal decor will not energetically fit here. However, meditation rooms for spiritual practices that supplant home office spaces will.

Family dynamics on the Neptune home line will tend to be supportive and deeply caring, though you may need to create boundaries.

PLU TO

Transformation | Power | Intensity
Rebirth | Revolution | Regeneration

The Pluto line signifies power places where you may experience the creative destruction of old behavioural patterns and negative ways of being. Not for the faint of heart, the Pluto line may require confrontation with hidden fears, the past, and darker impulses in order to arrive at a more profound place of self-understanding. While the intensity of the Pluto line can be challenging, it ultimately tends to provide opportunities for healing, spiritual development, and starting anew.

The Bulldozer Planet

One function of Pluto is that it breaks ground and brings forth radical new structures to collective life. Pluto also connects to the underground, as mythologically, Pluto is associated with Hades, the overlord of the afterlife who dwelled deep in the earth. This undergrounded-ness speaks to a somewhat scandalous quality to the Bulldozer Planet: its transits can dig up dirt or bring to light things we'd rather keep hidden, such as secrets, lies, fantasies, and hang-ups. Though Pluto moves slowly (the average lifespan will see Pluto move through roughly just a third of the zodiac), its movements signify big collective changes, as well as radical rebirth or fresh starts.

Pluto's Light Qualities

Ironically, the light side of this planet is that it activates our darker drives, obsessions, and the unconscious. Plutonic transformation often involves going through a dark phase to arrive at some new level of self-understanding. It can force us to face hard truths, to dig up memories long buried away in order to get beyond them.

Pluto's Shadow Qualities

Pluto can bring about momentous change for better or worse, meaning it has the potential to be a dark force. When Pluto transforms, it transforms on a grand, worldwide scale, changing systems first and our lives second, and revolutionizing the world and us with it. This energy can be complex and has the potential to be divisive, as one person's revolution can be another person's downfall.

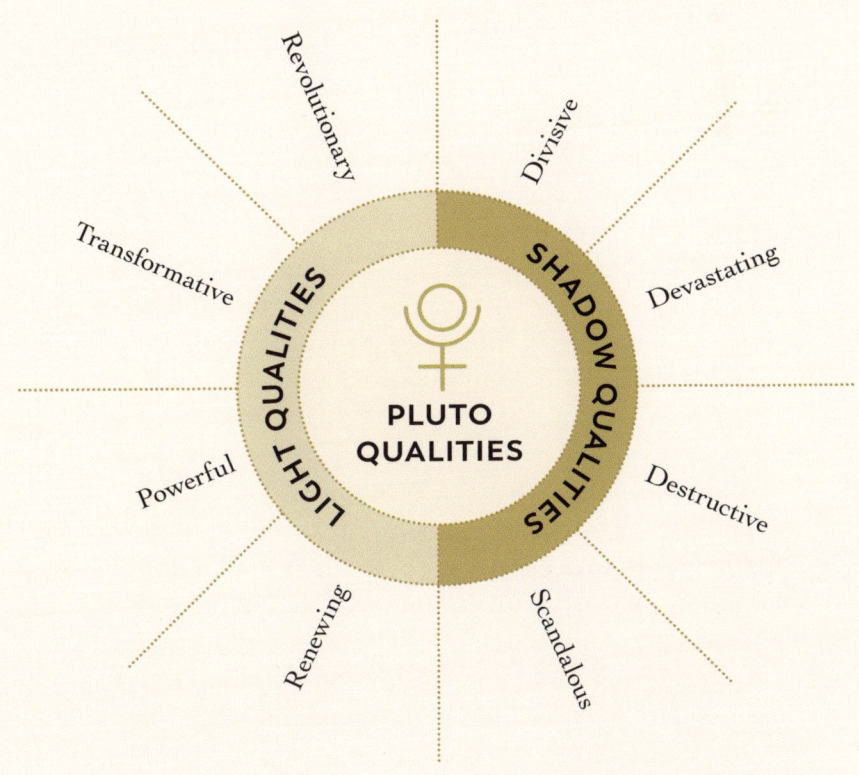

Life on the Pluto Line

Big. Explosive. Transformative. That's Pluto, and the Pluto line can be summarized by the word "power".

Life on the Pluto line can provide you with places where you can reclaim your power from someone or something that has taken it from you through trauma, harm, or dependency. It can also suggest places you may visit or relocate to when you've been overpowered by forces beyond your control. For example, no longer being able to deal with the monotony of marriage, mortgages, or middle management.

This line can also suggest power places upon which to carry out painful processing and redemption in solitude, and it's precisely the feeling of being alone that marks Pluto power places as sites of intense transformation and self-discovery.

You never know who you truly are until your life has stripped down to its basics, and those who reside on or visit their Pluto line typically find that their lives are ultimately infused with an eventual sense of purpose and empowerment, even if at first life on this line seems raw and bare. Ultimately, this can be a line for profound healing, recovery, and rebirth through confronting darkness.

BEST FOR
a health detox; fasting; purging; transforming; deep change; renewal; rebirth; intense experiences; healing; or seeking answers to deeper questions in life.

TRAVELLING ON YOUR PLUTO LINE

WHAT TO PLAN
visits to ancient sacred sites; a transformational retreat; or a deep healing experience like a plant medicine ceremony.

WHAT TO PACK
sage to burn to clear out the demons of the past; comforting items that provide emotional security, like a favourite blanket; black crystals like obsidian or black tourmaline to help ground and protect you; low-key outfits that allow you to focus on deep internal work; and a copy of G.W.F. Hegel's *The Phenomenology of Spirit*, a book about encountering the "night" of our inner negativity.

The Pluto
AC —————— Personal Line

The "dark night of the soul" – a phrase attributed to Spanish theologian and Christian mystic Saint John of the Cross – describes a journey through despair and self-doubt to transformation and rebirth. The dark night of the soul is a painful though necessary life transit where we are reduced to psychic destitution so that metamorphosis and maturity might ensue. And this concept accurately describes the impact of the Pluto personal line, which is one of our most intense lines.

This line is for those who know they need to change and heal from dark patterns. If you are looking to end up in a very different spiritual place to where you are in now, this line may be for you.

BE BRAVE

Expect fearless self-confrontation here, with
courage you may not have found on other lines.
This is where you dare to ask, "What have I become?"
in order to clear the path for the more empowered
question, "What will I become?"

EMBRACE SELF-HELP

Embrace any desires to improve or transform
yourself here. This can manifest in an interest in
ritual, the occult, or ascetic practices with an eye
towards purification of the past for new beginnings.

SWAP DESPAIR FOR HOPE

On this line, expect to emit a kind of inner
magnetism that comes with sacrificing old
ways of despair in favour of new ones of hope.

BREAK OLD HABITS

Expect to go beyond normal limits and
restraints here. This may mean doing the
necessary work to shatter old patterns
(especially if they are destructive).

The Pluto Relationship Line

DC ———

Relationships on the Pluto relationship line will be impossible to forget, and it is here that you will tend to attract your most intense loves. Some may leave scars, others may heal them, and while that can be the case with all romances, think of relationships here as an all-or-nothing proposition.

Relationships may be intense but short-lived on this line as you learn what you ultimately don't want. For those looking for a kind of fated and fatal attraction, this may be the line for you. But ultimately, the Pluto relationship line, while it might be a nice place to visit, may not be for living on, although you will likely emerge from romantic connections on this line looking at yourself in new ways, and surprised by your capacity for both deep love and, yes, even hate.

GET CO-CREATIVE

On other lines, love may be about personal completion. But on this line, it's not about completing each other, but about clearing out and building a new reality together that has nothing to do with the old coordinates of your self-concept.

MAKE UP AND BREAK UP

The intensity of this line can create the need for space, and then the longing for togetherness. In this topsy-turvy dynamic, expect an eventual desire for stability that relationships on this line may not afford.

BEWARE OF JEALOUS LOVERS

Here, you might attract partners who are powerful, assertive, and majestic, but who may force you to grapple with themes of control, jealousy, and trust. Or vice versa. Be careful out there and stay safe.

LOVE AS RUPTURE

The French philosopher Alain Badiou speaks of a kind of love that grips our being to such an extent that it ruptures the terms of the world we live in. Expect this kind of relationship here, where there is a radical break from the way things were before.

The Pluto
MC ——— Career Line

Pluto is connected to the underworld or things unseen. As such, you may be drawn to careers on this line where secrecy, confidentiality, and sensitive information matter. You may also be drawn to work that is highly transformative or that brings people from darkness to light. Remember, this is an extremely intense planetary line, so careers on it may deal in situations with life-altering consequences for those with whom you interact.

The Pluto career line may call for roles that will challenge you to uncover hidden truths or call the status quo into question. Once you begin looking behind the curtain, it's hard to stop, but this line will challenge you to do just that, as you search for truth and healing both for others and yourself.

FORGE NEW PATHS
While you may transform people's lives through work that requires intensity and urgency, another possibility on this line might be that you seek a career that radically breaks with your past work experience or expertise, as you forge a new path in search of rebirth.

BE A FORCE MULTIPLIER

On this line, turn projects and work structures inside out to make them more efficient, impactful, or game-changing. This might manifest by bringing your past experiences from an old career to a new one, creating friction and necessary change.

BE AUTHENTIC

Selling insurance is a respectable profession, but it may lack the authenticity needed in a more Plutonic career (say, helping displaced peoples find new lives in new lands). Look for a career that will confront real challenges, as they will empower you to confront yourself positively in turn.

CAREERS SUPPORTED BY PLUTO

PSYCHOLOGY	Careers in the field of psychotherapy and psychoanalysis align with Pluto's transformative energy by uncovering deep-seated issues.
END-OF-LIFE CARE PROVIDER	Careers in this zone of indeterminacy are particularly supported by the regenerative energy of Pluto.
REHABILITATION	Helping others work through addiction or pain aligns with Pluto's radically transformative power.
FORENSIC SCIENCE	Uncovering the hidden truths of crime scenes aligns with Pluto's penetrating and investigative nature.

The Pluto
Home Line

IC ———

We've all been to those homes where the resident's presence is so strong, hermetic, and private that we feel as though we're entering, with both trepidation and wonder, into an almost sacred space infused with some kind of medieval magic.

Living spaces on the Pluto home line will tend to feel like this, and are places where you may feel more at home than ever before, even if others who visit may feel less welcome, simply because the place is so undeniably yours. There is no Moon home line nourishment or Mercury bonhomie on this line. There is just you and maybe your family, growing like nightshade, unobserved, out of reach, and off limits to the world.

PROTECT YOUR PRIVACY

On this line, expect a home to feel more like a cloistered sanctuary. You may be more prone to retreat from the outside world on this line, with all the accoutrements that encourage solitude. Think landscaping and walls that ensure obscurity and distance, and window treatments that let in less Sun.

GROW IN THE DARK

The private feeling of the Pluto home line will allow you to grow in the mysterious and moody world of the interior spaces you've built. This is an excellent location to consider finishing a dissertation or long writing project.

SEEK HIDDEN SPACES

Pluto and secrecy go hand-in-hand, so try to find at least one hidden space just for you, like a garden, attic, a cellar passageway that leads to the Batmobile, or just a locked drawer where you can pen your obsessions far from the visibility of your partner.

REVEAL THE FAMILY SECRETS

Pluto digs up things that we may not want revealed, but that may lead to deeper understanding of a situation and reconciliation. On this line, expect these kinds of secrets to come to light, creating a home environment that may be challenging, but also liberating and healing.

> Living spaces on the Pluto home line are where you may feel more at home than ever before, because the place is undeniably yours.

REMOTE
ACTIVATION

Astrocartography from Afar

What if, logistically, you can't just jet to Lagos to enliven your Saturn career line? Or what if, financially, astrocartography seems beautiful to look at but impossible to touch? If you're in one of these scenarios, remote activation could be for you.

Remote activation means what it says: it's a subfield of astrocartography that allows you to benefit from power places by engaging or connecting with them from afar – kind of like a cosmic Zoom call. It might not be as great as visiting the actual place, but it's still something.

With remote activation, you may still experience the influence of a planetary line *in absentia*. Is Cairo great for romance, but you need to warm up more to the concept? This chapter details how you can bring power places to you, rather than the other way around.

The Mechanics of Remote Activation

Remote activation extends the precepts of astrocartography by positing that planetary influences need not stop at borders or city limits. Rather, remote activation holds that these planetary influences may be enlivened when you engage with people, ideas, languages, or institutions at a distance.

This notion of action at a distance shouldn't be hard to grasp, as astrology itself is a system of remote activation, based on the idea that planets act at distance from you, yet impact preferences, personality, and behavioural patterns.

Astrology and remote activation operate by way of a principle called energetic resonance. Everything in the universe – people, places, objects, and ideas – exist at specific frequencies. Remote activation occurs when, through some form of intentionality, ritual, or visualization, you create a resonance between your star map and your power place.

I like to think of astrocartography as a "Tinder for places", which matches you to your hotspots across the world. This includes remote activation, which functions by way of this resonance principle. While a remote match may not be as experientially fun as travelling or relocating to a power place, it may still be impactful for finding romance at-a-distance, or meeting a business contact that immeasurably alters your career path.

Many of my clients have used this notion of remote activation for a variety of reasons and to a variety of ends. For example, some will mobilize it for online dating by specifically filtering searches to power places auspicious for their relationship lines.

Activating Remotely

Say you're unable to travel much at present, but you're still interested in seeing what other power places might have to offer. This is where remote activation comes in. But what might that look like in terms of strategies and practical techniques?

We can think about remote activation through the lens of four main categories: visualization, immersion, virtual exploration, and incorporation. Each one traces out slightly different ways of bringing the energy of a power place closer to home.

VISUALIZATION

refers to practices where you meditate on or envision aspects of a power place to bring its influence into your life. For example, if a particular place feels like it's calling you, repeat a mantra that makes it feel as though you're already living here, like "I'm thriving in my dream job in Paris."

VIRTUAL EXPLORATION

makes use of profound advances in digital technologies, which allow you to connect with people and places through social media and other platforms. This category aims to increase a particular planetary line's influence by engaging with a power place online.

THE FOUR REMOTE ACTIVATION CATEGORIES

INCORPORATION

is all about bringing objects linked to a power place into your personal space to increase energetic resonance. These objects may be gleaned from things that have caught your eye during virtual explorations or while researching through immersion. Such objects will remind you of where you are planning to go, before you even get there.

IMMERSION

refers to practices where you come to know all about a power place and its culture, history, and traditions. The more you immerse yourself in the unique contours of a place, the more you enliven its energy. Immersion techniques would involve taking classes, reading books, or going to libraries to research one of your power places.

Remotely Activating Personal Lines

Your personal lines point to locations where you may feel more energized on your journey towards self-discovery and transformation. Here are some ideas for bringing the power of a place with all its cosmic support into your life through remote activation.

TAKE ACTION
Align with the hustle or low-key energy of a power place by matching activities to it. If one of your hotspots on your personal line is known for its cosmopolitanism, heighten your sense of culture to match. If your line crosses through a spiritual locale, engage in meditation, yoga, or other practices that help visualize yourself thriving in that place.

EXCHANGE CULTURE
Learn about a place's approach to self-expression, identity, or personal growth to gain insights into how you can respectfully and authentically incorporate those values into your life. Through virtual exploration or immersion you can better embody the nuances of a location.

SPEAK UP
Frankish monarch Charlemagne famously said, "To have a second language is to possess a second soul." Language acquisition that aligns with a power place will enliven your second soul by immersing yourself in, and, incorporating its language.

FIND NEW STYLES
Activate a power place remotely by finding a look that resonates with you, and that you can respectfully incorporate. Check out influencers and fashion mavens from locations on your chosen personal line to help guide and update your wardrobe.

Remotely Activating Relationship Lines

Some of my clients use filter-based online dating search functions to hone potential romantic connections based on their power places, and so can you. Your Venus relationship line goes through Melbourne? Filter your search around Australia's finest city (sorry, Perth). If this isn't for you, there are also other less technologically mediated remote activation methods, too.

GO CULTURE CLUBBING

Is one of your power places for romance in New Zealand? See if there are any clubs and cultural centres near to you that provide expats refuge and reconnection to their home country, language, and traditions. You may find an unexpected relationship there.

SPEAK THE (LOVE) LANGUAGE

People express themselves differently in different places. This obviously pertains not only to language, but the way a culture says things. An understatement here, a passionate confessional there. Learn the cadences of your chosen power place so your word can become your emotional bond with a romantic partner from afar.

EXPLORE THE FRIEND ZONE

Relationships aren't just about romance, and, crucially, the relationship line isn't either. Friendships also fall under its rubric. Look for people online or at local cultural events from your power places to help you better understand the ins and outs of the culture. Plus, it's always key to have a good travel buddy for when you finally visit one of your hotspots.

Remotely Activating Career Lines

Your career lines probably offer the clearest instance of how remote activation may work for you. Like astrology, so much of business is all about action at a distance. Wheeling and dealing on your planetary career lines from afar may very well yield dividends, best-in-class solutions, and optimized revenue streams for your brand or side hustle.

FIND A VIRTUAL MENTOR
Seek out virtual mentorship from individuals in your field and on your chosen career line so you can learn and prosper from bespoke mentorship aligned to a power place.

GET AD SAVVY
If you run your own business, target ads for your brand based around your astrocartography lines and specify exactly which locations you want your ads to run in. Using remote activation to cherry pick where your budget goes may furnish better returns than randomly suggesting all of America for an ad.

ACT REMOTELY, WORK REMOTELY
If you're open to remote work, targeting jobs or applying to positions along your career lines can be highly effective. Virtual exploration and visualization will be helpful here, too, as you think about which companies might best align with your values.

DEVELOP PASSION PROJECTS
Use remote activation techniques to develop projects in line with your true passions. Dive into research and use that inspiration to fuel your side hustle, as the career line is deeply connected to how you want to impact the world.

Remotely Activating Home Lines

Your home lines suggest places for nurturing and grounding energy, allowing you to feel more emotionally balanced and connected to your immediate surroundings. If you are out of joint or unsettled in your living environment, remote activation of home line energy can provide a stabilizing influence no matter where you are.

BRING THE OUTSIDE IN

If your chosen home line runs through a space known for its nature, incorporate flora, scents, or sounds that resonate with its natural history. By surrounding yourself with artefacts, objects, sounds, or symbols on your home lines, you enable the resonance principle.

SEE IT

Visualize or meditate on a power place on your chosen home line to mentally take you there. This could also involve working with a specific mantra or affirmation that connects to the themes of home, ancestry, the past, and emotional security.

GOOGLE IT

Use virtual maps to navigate streets, museums, clubs, landmarks, and other institutions related to your power place through virtual exploration, and get to know a place from afar.

FEED YOUR SOUL

The home line is all about emotional nourishment. Join a local cooking class to feed your mind, body, and soul with traditional cuisine from a power place. Such immersive practices provide a profound means to align with a given culture remotely.

Mind Your Planets

The previous pages gave general techniques for remote activation, but you should also keep in mind that each planetary line will have a specific flavour, aim, and energy. So, while these practical techniques provide a general framework for remote activation, you will always want to pay attention to which planet's energy you are enlivening through the resonance principle.

For example, if you're focusing on remotely activating your Venus personal line through social media, for example, people will likely perceive you as charming, sweet, and pleasant. On the other hand, if you're activating your Mars personal line, you might come across as assertive or intense.

Similarly, if your career line runs through the location of a particular company's headquarters, it can bring you additional luck and opportunities when it comes to investing in them remotely. However, as always, heed the particular planets you're remotely activating. Slow and serious Saturn, for example, would imply a long-term return on your investment. If you are willing to wait, no problem. Jupiterian energy, of course, would be a lot more beneficial for "quick wins".

Using Transits

A further way to intensify the impact of remote activation is through planetary transits. Transits refer to planetary movements happening in the sky right now, and these movements can help you determine when the good times are coming, and when the not so good ones are.

For example, every 12 years, we will experience a Jupiter return. This is a particularly auspicious transit, during which time we may enjoy more love, income, or opportunity in our lives, making this a great time to work with your Jupiter line.

To track your transits, you will need to pay attention to the stars, so read your horoscope or set up a personal consultation with an astrologer. You can also do some basic tracking following a few rules of thumb. By understanding these, you will already be taking crucial steps towards intensifying your remote activation.

THE TWO RULES TO TRACKING TRANSITS

RULE ONE

Even in the middle of winter, birthdays are always sunny, astrologically speaking, because for about 30 days around your birthday (see page 31–33 for when these dates fall based on your star sign), the Sun will be super strong in your chart. Celebrate each birthday by remotely activating or visiting places on your Sun lines.

RULE TWO

Avoid remote activation during retrograde transits. A retrograde refers to when a planet seems to be moving backwards in the sky relative to us on Earth. When this happens, a planet's influence gets all wonky. Mars retrogrades are notorious for making us feel cooped up, while Mercury retrogrades can interrupt travel plans.

Notable Transits

☉ **SOLAR RETURN**
A time for personal empowerment, vitality, and new beginnings.

☿ **MERCURY RETROGRADE**
Can cause communication and travel complications.

♀ **VENUS DIRECT**
Enhances love, relationships, beauty, and finances.

☾ **LUNAR ECLIPSE**
Can bring uncertainty and emotional shifts.

♂ **MARS DIRECT**
Energizes assertive action and bold moves.

♃ **JUPITER RETURN**
A more abundant time to travel for opportunities and growth.

♄ **SATURN DIRECT AND RETROGRADE**
Brings structure, discipline, and karmic lessons.

♅ **URANUS DIRECT AND RETROGRADE**
Brings sudden change, innovation, and liberation.

♆ **NEPTUNE DIRECT AND RETROGRADE**
Unveils hidden truths, inspiring spiritual journeys.

♇ **PLUTO DIRECT AND RETROGRADE**
Can bring powerful transformation for better or worse.

BUILDING YOUR ITINERARY

Planning Your Trip

Before I got into astrocartography, whenever I planned a trip, it would look like this: I'd check my bank account and randomly make hasty plans with a friend based on my financial situation. If I was flush with cash, the trip might involve a plane and resort hotel. If I wasn't, it usually entailed onerous road tripping, budget hotels or sleeping bags, and many bad moods, as we'd get lost using outdated maps leading to dead-ends in Bavarian mountain towns. Never did these trips make use of astrocartography, and in retrospect, I wish they had.

Now, whenever I plan an itinerary, I do so with intention and my star map. Instead of randomly choosing a place to go or looking up most popular destinations, I let my cosmic map guide me.

In this chapter, we will look at some example itineraries, which is less about picking a place and more about aligning with a cosmically resonant destination. Even if you're planning your itinerary on a budget with astrocartography, take comfort in the knowledge that it's being bank-rolled by the largesse of the stars.

Travelling with Intention

When you're planning your next adventure, ask yourself: what kind of energy do I need right now? Is it love and beauty, or is it the fiery drive of ambition? Do you want to open up new intellectual horizons and finally tackle *The Hegel's Phenomenology of Spirit*, or dive deep into a personal transformation? With astrocartography, your travels become, in a part, a reflection of your needs.

If, for example, there are places you've always felt drawn to, start there. Many find that their astrocartography lines often align with destinations they've long been fascinated by or feel an unexplainable pull toward. There's likely a reason for that – the planets in your chart may already be guiding you towards these powerful, energetic connections.

Just make sure you are practical about things. If you're looking at a Jupiter line and debating between a destination that's a two-hour flight away versus one that is 12 hours away, why not start with the closer one? Be savvy with your outlays by taking costs into the equation, and if you must choose between two lines and budget is an issue, choose the way that makes the most sense for you.

An Example Itinerary

Let's bring this concept to life with real-world examples of how to use your planetary lines to plan your dream trip. Each planet brings a unique energy to the table, and the key is matching your destination with your goals.

One of my absolute favourite go-to lines for fun is Uranus, and the best way I can think to help you craft your perfect itinerary for it is by explaining it through one of my favourite TV shows.

One of the best *Seinfeld* episodes is called "The Opposite", in which nebbish George Costanza, the show's heel, decides to break with every routine he has followed in his life. Instead of his usual order of tuna on toast, coleslaw, and a cup of coffee, he does the opposite, or unexpected, and goes with chicken salad on rye, untoasted, with a side of potato salad, and a cup of tea.

Despite Jerry's protestation that, technically, chicken salad isn't the opposite of tuna, an attractive woman overhears George's order (which is the same as hers) and looks in his direction. He approaches her (the opposite of his instincts) and tells her that he is unemployed and lives with his parents. She's instantly smitten and they go on a date, while he also ends up getting his dream job with the American baseball team, the New York Yankees.

A holiday on the Uranus line might look something like opposite day for you. Here, ordering your own version of chicken salad on rye will be cosmically supported, leading potentially to unexpected romances and your version of working with the Yankees. At the same time, this might also be a line to visit if you're looking to enliven a spirit of anti-establishment activism or engage in work that seeks to redress inequalities to create a more just and equal cosmic order. Such a spirit of rebellion will tend to manifest here.

Your Unpredictable Holiday

DESTINATION: YOUR URANUS AC LINE

Day 1
EMBRACE OPPOSITES DAY

Never dreamt of asking for an upgrade at the hotel? Do it anyway. Uranus wants you to jump out of your comfort zone and trust that the chaos is part of the fun. Do something you'd never normally do on this first day of your wildcard trip.

Day 2
DITCH THE ITINERARY

This is not the time to be the person with a laminated schedule. Wander. Get lost. Ask locals for tips. Say yes to whatever feels right in the moment. Uranus doesn't like rules, and honestly, neither should you.

Day 3
BE SPONTANEOUS

Book something like a last-minute event or excursion, like a last-minute ticket to a midnight art show.

Day 4
REINVENT YOURSELF

Go shopping for clothes that make you feel like someone else entirely. Buy the jacket with spikes or that dress that's more sculpture than fabric.

Day 5
SEEK OUT THE WEIRD & WONDERFUL

Forget the standard art museum. On this last day of your trip, find an exhibit that makes people say, "I don't get it". Skip the romcom and watch something surreal and Lynchian. This is the energy of groundbreaking creativity.

Navigating Conflicting Planetary Lines with Others

We all have unique astrocartography maps, so while it's possible for you and your friends to share lines in common, it's rare for everyone to have the same Venus line running through a particular place. With a little planning, this is where astrocartography becomes a fun and collaborative experience.

What if your dream destination is on your partner's Mars line, but on your Venus line? No problem. Just mix the magic of both planets! While you soak up the luxury and indulgence of Venusian activities, your partner can dive into high-energy adventures and action-packed experiences. Embrace the fun of blending relaxation with excitement, and carve out days for each of you to fully enjoy your planetary vibes.

TIPS FOR NAVIGATING CONFLICTING PLANETARY LINES WITH A PARTNER

MIX ACTIVITIES
Combine activities that cater to both of your planetary influences.

SCHEDULE IN PERSONAL TIME
Allow for individual activities that are aligned with your respective lines.

COMMUNICATE AND COMPROMISE
Discuss and balance both of your expectations.

EMBRACE DIFFERENCES
Use the opportunity to try exciting new experiences together.

Example Itinerary Balancing Venus and Mars Energies

	MORNING	AFTERNOON	EVENING
Day 1	A hike (Mars)	Art gallery (Venus)	Spa treatment (Venus)
Day 2	Skydiving (Mars)	A beauty treatment (Venus)	A romantic dinner (Venus)
Day 3	Scenic bike ride (Mars and Venus)	Sculpture park (Venus)	Wine tasting (Venus)

Trip Planning for Couples and Families

As a consultant for couples and families, I often look at maps for multiple people to find a destination that offers the best overall experience for all. While it's unlikely to find a place that perfectly aligns with everyone's lines, the goal is to find a location that offers a balance of positive energies for all.

Plan a trip with a destination where each of you has a different planetary line running through. Maybe one of you has a Mars line, another has Mercury, and someone else has Venus. It's like creating an astrological dream team. Once you've picked the spot, give each person the task of organizing an activity based on their planetary energy, which can look something like this:

The Uranus child can handle the surprises and suggest an out-of-the-ordinary activity to shake things up.

The person with the Venus line can plan the fun stuff, like indulgent meals, nights out, and anything centred around beauty and pleasure.

The person with the Mercury line can handle all the travel plans, making sure logistics are smooth.

The person working with their Mars line can be in charge of any action-packed activities like a group hike, a fitness class, or something that gets everyone moving.

If someone has a Moon line, they can take charge of booking a day trip that feels nurturing, cosy, and zen.

Conclusion

We began this astrocartography journey speaking about the "importance of elsewhere". We end by talking about home. It may seem an odd place to land, given that we have spent this whole book looking out into the world to find where you might better live and thrive. But, by helping you locate your power places, astrocartography brings you into closer contact with your cosmic self, and, in this sense, it takes you homeward to where destiny and destination are one. It suggests that your connection to the world is more than a matter of chance; rather, it is influenced by the planetary energies that ground your existence. These lines on your map represent not just geographical locations but sacred spaces that resonate with your soul's moral and spiritual compass.

Through the mini-journey that was reading this book, you have now gained the insights necessary to navigate decisions for travel, relocation, and remote activation, based on your unique star map. You have seen how our planets are more than distant, indifferent objects, but instead embodiments of fundamental archetypal energies that we all interact with in various ways. By coming to know these planetary influences, you can now better appreciate the roles these archetypes play in your own life.

Ultimately, in learning how to read your star map, you have gained the knowledge and techniques necessary to orient yourself towards your personalized sites of power and abundance – and thereby the greater cosmic whole. You have learned, in other words, to be at home in the world.

It is my prayer, then, that even if you knew little about astrology or astrocartography when you picked this book up, you can now engage with your maps for inspiration, direction, and guidance. As you embark on your travels, use this book as an almanac for the exploration of both the external world and your internal landscape.

As I write these words on my Saturn line in Ireland, the same strange country Philip Larkin visits in his poem about the "importance of elsewhere", I must take a moment in the end to express a final gratitude to my loved ones who have all helped guide me when the stars could not, and, of course, to you, dear reader, for taking this book seriously, the writing of which has been its own remarkable journey.

Index

Recommended Resources

Here's a curated list of books, art, and films to evoke the essence of each planet.

THE SUN

Klara and the Sun by Kazuo Ishiguro explores the nature of selfhood as Klara, a solar-powered "artificial friend," learns what it means to be human, and is energized by the life-giving force of the Sun.

THE MOON

Soul Under the Moon, an exhibition by Yayoi Kusama, is a must see to align with the Moon's emotional nature.

MERCURY

Daft Punk's high octane *Discovery* provides the most appropriate soundtrack to the dynamic, shapeshifting energy of Mercury.

VENUS

Portrait of a Lady on Fire, directed by Céline Sciamma, is a powerful film about a forbidden, same-sex romance that evokes the sensuous, intimate energy of Venus.

MARS

The Art of War by Sun Tzu perfectly embodies Mars's spirit. Align with Mars by keying into Sun Tzu's insights on calculated force, discipline, and tactics.

JUPITER

Align with Jupiter with Chimamanda Ngozi Adichie's *Americanah*, a novel that explores opportunity and identity and captures the elation of chance to be found on a path towards a new destiny.

SATURN
Nothing embodies Saturn's energy (orderly, structured, minimal) quite like the austere modern architecture, examples of which can be seen in Peter Carter's classic book *Mies van der Rohe at Work*.

URANUS
Eraserhead by David Lynch is unique, strange, and captivating, and is one of the closest things we have to align with Uranus energy.

NEPTUNE
The Waves by Virginia Woolf is a dreamlike novel that follows the lives of six characters, exploring their inner lives. Written in a stream of consciousness, it is much like the influence of Neptune.

PLUTO
The album *Monoliths and Dimensions* by Sunn O))) is a vast masterwork of glacial drone-scapes that create a sense of being drawn into Pluto's underworld of hidden realms and dark truths.

About the Author

Clarisse Monahan is the founder of Venus in Retrograde, which provides astrology-focused services from one-on-one consultations to team-building and brand activations. She has written extensively on the intersection of astrology, politics, and culture for numerous publications, and is the resident astrologer for Soho House worldwide, where she lectures on astrological topics, both general and specific.

Photo by Kieran Behan

Acknowledgments

DK would like to thank Francesco Piscitelli for proofreading and Vanessa Bird for indexing.

The publisher would also like to thank the following for their kind permission to reproduce their photographs:

(Key: a-above; b-below/bottom; c-centre; f-far; l-left; r-right; t-top)

9 Unsplash: Laura Vinck. 13 Alamy Stock Photo: Science History Images. 19 Shutterstock.com: Kanok Sulaiman. 21 Getty Images / iStock: Bjdlzx. 24 Unsplash: Filmplusdigital. 30 Dreamstime.com: Fabio Lamanna. 34 Unsplash: Toa Heftiba. 37 Getty Images: Johner Images. 60 Unsplash: Lili Kovac. 63 Unsplash: Nappy. 66 Unsplash: Johan Mouchet. 74 Getty Images / iStock: Oleh Slobodeniuk. 77 Getty Images / iStock: Ernest Fontsere Cuni. 81 Unsplash: Luz Brunetti. 88 Unsplash: Kinga Howard. 91 Getty Images: Cyndi Monaghan. 94 Unsplash: Daniel J Schwarz. 103 Getty Images / iStock: MStudioImages. 105 Unsplash: Alexander McFeron. 109 Getty Images / iStock: Hobo_018. 116 Getty Images: Westend61. 119 Unsplash: Everton Vila. 130 Unsplash: Gaelle Marcel. 132 Dreamstime.com: F Baarssen. 144 Unsplash: Becca Schultz. 147 Getty Images: WHL. 159 Unsplash: Micha Bielejewski. 160 Getty Images / iStock: Oleh Slobodeniuk. 172 Getty Images / iStock: Paolo Graziosi. 175 Getty Images / iStock: Gang Zhou. 178 Dreamstime.com: Wirestock. 186 Getty Images / iStock: Ian Mcdonnell. 189 Getty Images: Tim Robberts. 198 Unsplash: Ravi Pinisetti. 204 Getty Images / iStock: Will Tudor. 211 Unsplash: Benjamin Voros. 214 Unsplash: Reinhart ‧Julian. 216 Getty Images / iStock: Pixdeluxe. 219 Getty Images / iStock: Wildroze. 223 Kieran Behan

Senior Aquisitions Editor Zara Anvari
Aquisitions Editor Amy Slack
Senior Designer Jordan Lambley
Senior Production Editor Tony Phipps
Senior Production Controller Luca Bazzoli
DTP & Design Coordinator Heather Blagden
Publishing Assistant Emily Cannings
Art Director Maxine Pedliham
Publishing Director Stepanie Jackson

Editorial Chloe Murphy
Design Hart Studio
Illustration Dan Crisp
Picture Research Claire Guest

First published in Great Britain in 2025 by Dorling Kindersley Limited, 20 Vauxhall Bridge Road, London SW1V 2SA

The authorised representative in the EEA is Dorling Kindersley Verlag GmbH. Arnulfstr. 124, 80636 Munich, Germany

Text copyright © Clarisse Monahan 2025
Copyright © 2025 Dorling Kindersley Limited
A Penguin Random House Company
10 9 8 7 6 5 4 3 2 1
001–349251–Sep/2025

Printed and bound in China

www.dk.com

MIX
Paper | Supporting responsible forestry
FSC™ C018179
www.fsc.org

This book was made with Forest Stewardship Council™ certified paper – one small step in DK's commitment to a sustainable future. Learn more at www.dk.com/uk/information/sustainability